American Revolution: Soldier Motivations

Georgianna T. Roberts

Abstract

In this comparative social history of the American Revolution, the stories of eight men are recounted through the use of their biographies, journals, and memoirs. The lives of four enlisted soldiers and four officers are depicted to gain an understanding of how they became involved in the revolution. In order to do so, their early lives are scrutinized, as well as their post-war lives as they transitioned to peacetime. The main purpose, however, is to examine how each man became motivated to join the war for independence, whether socially, economically, and/or politically. As each man had different aspirations for their expectations before and after the war, one thing is certain: the enlisted soldiers were motivated for different reasons compared to the officers.

By examining their early lives, as well as post-war lives, one can gain a better understanding of whether their motivations came to fruition, in the end. The intention is not to disprove their patriotism or zeal for joining the war, but instead to prove there were other motivational factors that contributed to their decision. Their patriotism is undeniable, which was a crucial reason why they were able to win the war after eight long years. Even though they experienced deprivation for eight years, due to the lack of resources, the spirit of the men could not be deterred. Despite harrowing circumstances, the revolutionary soldiers were able to prevail over a superior enemy. With that, their motivations and expectations must be examined to shed light on how these men were able to win the war.

Table of Contents

Introduction

The American Revolution united a group of people who were striving for independence against Great Britain and no longer felt no need to be dependent upon the "mother-country." Dependence was an option no more for the group of ordinary men who sought to formulate their own government based on their own principles. For a revolution to succeed there must be substantial grievances that are felt by many people. It takes shared ideas as to what is wrong, what needs to be done, and what a better future may look like. There also must be coalitions that require different sorts of people who have organization, direction, and discipline. The task was to get ordinary Americans to generate a new social and political consciousness. The revolution was able to emerge from confrontation politics in which ordinary citizens began joining popular movements. The American people knew what was at stake: power, just ideas, interest, property, and the course of the future.

Ordinary people began envisioning the benefits of independence and no longer being "loyal subjects to the King." This process inadvertently created a class system where the upper echelon gained a sense of entitlement. The lower echelon, on the other hand, constantly battled "to influence, not dominate, politics," as historian Gary Nash poignantly suggests. [1] The lower classes began to search for an opportunity to alleviate their socioeconomic struggles. New England, however, dealt with what Nash refers to as the "narrowing of opportunities and the rise of poverty." [2] This led to New England becoming the epicenter for revolt in America.

Lower class individuals were losing the battle to be involved politically in America. The American Revolution, however, provided them with a new sense of opportunity to prove they were equal to the upper class. The historian Eric Robson notes "the Revolution was the work of an active minority which persuaded a hesitant majority to a cause for which that majority had very little real enthusiasm." [3] The revolution created opportunities socially, politically, and economically for the lower class, while the upper class pondered their involvement in the war. In short, the lower class became radicals and their ideology won over the masses with the goal being independence.

In this comparative study, the focus will be on how both classes became involved in the revolutionary conflict. How ordinary men were motivated for such a conflict that must have seemed impossible is a significant aspect to the revolution. Both classes were influenced socially, politically, and economically, but in different ways. Exploring the motivations between why private soldiers-generally lower class-and officers-generally upper class-joined the war effort is just the beginning. These men took full advantage of the revolution to forge paths that would contribute to their own self-interests. Next, examining their expectations before and after the war will become essential to this study. By exploring their motivations and expectations, it will become clearer as to how the revolutionary soldiers and officers perceived the War for Independence. Their sense of mission and national identity will also become clearer. The different driving motivational forces for each class will help one to understand the revolution and how the contemporaries viewed their positions within society.

There were several motivational forces that enabled the colonists to gain a sense of national identity. Americans were serving what historian Charles Royster calls a "godly purpose" as they were fighting for self-preservation. [4] If self-preservation became a failure, there would be nothing left for the Americans to fight for. The Americans had an innate desire to stay alive and the acceptance of death enabled the soldiers to stand up to tyranny. Religion had become a major factor in motivating the colonists to declare independence.

The Great Awakening had enlightened the revolutionaries as they believed their permanent independence rested with God because he would ensure their virtue and destiny. The revolutionaries believed that "death in obedience to God and in service to the public meant a soul at peace." [5] They feared being enslaved by the British, and they sacrificed their lives to ensure that was not an option. Essentially, Americans believed it was their duty to gain redemption for the world and become what Royster calls "God's instruments to smash tyranny." [6] Their sense of mission was to create a perfect utopian world and an "uncorrupted promise land." [7]

The religious revival motivated and invited many revolutionaries to seek a better opportunity to become socially mobile in a growing society. The colonists wanted to be free and independent without being oppressed by British control. That sentiment alone was enough motivation for most men to join the revolutionary cause.

The revolutionaries also could not envision their lives, as well as their families and estates being regularly controlled by British parliamentary taxes. Royster notes that "Americans needed reason to believe that resistance could succeed" and that success was inevitable. [8] Throughout the war, there was a sentiment among these soldiers and officers that their faith in American destiny would prevail. "The survival of the Continental Army," Royster contends, "would depend not only on American soldiers' public spirit and combat prowess, but also on the army's routine ability to keep men healthy, to keep them from killing each other, and to cheat them no more than they would tolerate." [9] It was the duty of the officer to keep the men under control, but many officers were just as young and naïve as the private soldiers. The private soldiers often realized they were equal to the officers, but were forced to defer to their leadership.

This study will also focus on what motivated both, the common soldier and the officers, to join the revolution - each for different reasons - with one common theme emerging between them. These revolutionaries joined the army based on their own personal circumstances, such as advancement in society and economic growth. For the most part, these soldiers were opportunistic in their approach when joining the army. Of course, they wanted to defend their country, but more importantly they saw an opportunity to manipulate the army to better their own social standing within society. These "urban people," writes Gary Nash, "upset the equilibrium of an older system of social relations and turned the seaport towns into crucibles of revolutionary agitation." [10] The motivation for the lowest ranking groups wanted to prove they were equal to the upper ranks of colonial society.

By 1775, the New England colonies became vastly transformed. The people were no longer "working harmoniously for the mutual good of the whole society." [11] Instead, a political consciousness had emerged among the ordinary people in colonial New England that was based on competing for their own self-interests. A complex class structure developed, which was shaped by economic and social struggle. Gary Nash describes this struggle as when "urban people gradually came to think of themselves as belonging to economic groups that did not share common goals, began to behave in class specific ways in response to events that impinged upon their well-being, and manifested ideological points of view and cultural characteristics peculiar to their rank." [12] The lowest ranks of society began developing a political consciousness as they struggled to get ahead. The highest ranks of society believed their standing was justified by wealth and education. They believed it was their duty to lead and those at the bottom should defer to their superior wisdom and wealth. It was believed widely by those at the top that those at the bottom should accept their lowly positions which were divinely willed.

The problems only persisted after the war for the common soldier. The transition to peacetime became a struggle for most as the war had claimed their youthful days. It became apparent that the army had manipulated the individuals who participated, which disappointed the soldiers after the war. The officers appeared to fare better in their social and political standing than the common soldier. The officers had known men of high rank and used those connections to obtain positions within society and the government. Private soldiers had a difficult time preparing for their future because most were young and saw the army as their place of employment. When the dissolution of the army occurred shortly after the war, it left those men contemplating their next moves.

By examining the highest and lowest ranks of society as they joined the war for independence, one can understand their motives and expectations with more clarity. The lowest members of society generally enlisted for the war effort to get off the bottom of society. They were motivated socially and economically to attain their own self-interests. Joseph Plumb Martin, John Greenwood, George Robert Twelves Hewes, and Jeremiah Greenman were men who manipulated the revolution for their own self-preservation. [13] These men joined the war for various reasons, but one common occurrence emerged between these revolutionaries. Each man joined with the notion that they were searching for opportunity in a country that offered little. Essentially, these men viewed the war as an opportunity to elevate their status within society.

Other men, such as Colonel Benjamin Tallmadge, Lt. Benjamin Gilbert, General William Barton, and Captain Stephen Olney had a choice as to whether they would join the war. [14] Their elevated social status allowed them to contemplate whether they would fight for independence. Each of these men had various opportunities in America that did not involve risking their own lives. These men were motivated for different reasons than the lowest ranks of society, but joined based off their own self-interests. The army offered them the opportunity to lead men into battle based on their own education and superior wisdom. In short, the army essentially became the scapegoat for the revolutionaries of both ranks of society to achieve their own interests.

Each of these men provides significant information towards their motives for joining the army, their hardships, and the transition to peacetime. It is imperative to gain a complete understanding of how these men with their conflicting motives were able to coexist and win the war. These men were simply inspired to create a new world based on opportunity. This comparative study will begin by examining the social standing of each person's family. In the first chapter, these types of questions need to be addressed: What type of childhood did they have? Did they get an education? Did they learn any type of trade? Was there an opportunity, outside of war, for them? What were they leaving behind? What was the standard of living in their respective New England colonies? The answers to these questions will solidify their motivations and expectations after the war.

The second and third chapters will focus on the private soldiers and the officers. These chapters will examine their motivations for joining the war and how their wartime experiences changed their way of thinking. It is also imperative to examine if there is any type of national identity or sense of mission that developed as they joined the war. The motives for these men will be scrutinized as it was not a necessity for some to join the war. It can be argued that the soldiers often experienced more deprivation than the officers during the war. This appears to have become an underlying motivational factor for the soldiers as they were constantly in a state of proving they were equal to the officers. The fourth chapter will consist of describing their transition to peacetime and how they differed.

Some questions that need to be answered throughout this study are as follows: Were they expecting any type of recognition for fighting in the war? Were they expecting to obtain social or political standing within society? Were they disappointed with the government? Were their motives of the highest and noblest kind (mostly referring to the officers)? The latter question is referring to individualism amongst the selected officers for this study. In short, these questions will help to substantiate how they perceived the War for Independence and how they were able to coexist in a competitive society.

This study will expound upon Gary Nash's *The Urban Crucible: Social Change, Political Consciousness, and the Origins of the American Revolution* (1979)[15] and Charles Royster's *A Revolutionary People at War: the Continental Army and American Character, 1775-1783* (1979).[16] The intention of this study is largely to show how each social class was able to win the war, despite their different motivations for joining the war. Comprehending how men of different classes contributed to the war is vital to understanding the revolution to its fullest.

The different classes that emerged with various personalities and motives can explain how the revolutionaries viewed the Revolution. The success of the revolution would come from the desire of each class, who were seeking their own self-interests. This study will provide a glimpse into the lives of various soldiers who were faced with life altering decisions. It can be argued that the early eighteenth century theory of "working harmoniously together for the mutual good of society" could have thwarted American success. America needed a competitive society to push one another towards its highest goal: liberty.

[1] Gary B. Nash, *The Urban Crucible: Social Change, Political Consciousness, and the Origins of the American Revolution* (Cambridge: Harvard University Press, 1979), 264.

[2] Ibid., ix.

[3] Eric Robson, *In It's Political and Military Aspects, 1763-1783* (New York: De Capo Press, 1972), 41.

[4] Charles Royster, *A Revolutionary People at War: the Continental Army and American Character, 1775-1783* (Chapel Hill: University of North Carolina Press, 1979), 15.

[5] Ibid., 17.

[6] Ibid., 152.

[7] Ibid., 154.

[8] Ibid., 9.

[9] Ibid., 83.

[10] Nash, *The Urban Crucible*, viii.

[11] Ibid., 384.

[12] Ibid., x.

[13] These four common soldiers were chosen for this study because they dealt with narrowing opportunities that caused them to join a war that had the potential to offer socioeconomic standing within the New England colonies.

[14] These four officers were chosen for this study because they were not forced to join the American cause in the Revolution. They were afforded opportunity outside of joining a war that threatened their lives. However, each of these men joined with carefully articulated goals of advancement within society. These men were seeking political and economic standing in their respective New England colonies. Their standing would only be enhanced as distinguished military officers of the American Revolution.

[15] Nash analyzes how people in the eighteenth century developed a growing political consciousness and how class relationships shifted to a competitive society.

[16] Royster examines what Americans believed the war would create for their future and why they felt they could succeed against a superior opponent.

Chapter 1

Pre-Revolution: Early Life and Standard of Living for Eight Men

Colonial America transformed from the pursuit of the common good to a socially and economically competitive society. By the 1770s, the revolution was beginning to take shape and many had to make a decision that would impact their lives forever. The revolution in New England offered ordinary men an opportunity to develop a social and political consciousness. This new type of consciousness enabled these men to influence society in a revolutionary way, and contributed to a mass social upheaval that provided new opportunity for the lower class.

One member of the lowest rank was Joseph Plumb Martin. Martin's story began in Berkshire County, Massachusetts where he was born on November 21, 1760 (supposedly Thanksgiving). His father, Ebenezer Martin, was the son of a "substantial New England farmer." [17] When Ebenezer realized that he could not endure manual labor for an occupation he enrolled at Yale College between 1750 and 1755. Ebenezer was able to get an education as he searched for opportunity. He eventually became a Gospel Minister of the Congregational Order, but was constantly at odds with some parishes because of his unorthodox opinions. His mother was a farmer's daughter, born in New Haven County, Connecticut. His father's lifestyle and opinions led Martin to moving to Milford, Connecticut, at age seven, with his maternal grandparents.

Connecticut was a large agricultural center unlike the urban cities of Boston, New York, and Philadelphia. It was not an urban-dominated society, but provided opportunity for those who sought employment outside of farming, such as being an artisan or merchant. However, like most colonies, those opportunities dwindled for many. Connecticut suffered from a constant shortage of currency as there was an "unfavorable balance of trade with England, newcomers' bringing with them goods rather than money, and the laws of Parliament, which forbade export of coin to the colonies and coinage of money there." [18] However, by the eve of the revolution, Connecticut's economy had improved. The colony benefited from increased trade and an increased amount of goods, enabling Connecticut and its people to have flexibility in choosing their way of life.

Before the 1760s, Connecticut was self-governed, which enabled them to have rights that other colonies did not. They were loyal to the king, but the king did not appoint a governor for Connecticut and royal patronage did not operate within the colony. Essentially, Connecticut had the right to make its own laws, unlike most other colonies. Connecticut also felt no obligation to become involved in a war or separate from the mother country until it felt threatened. This threat became a reality with the revenue acts of the 1760s and 1770s that forced Connecticut to "preserve its ancient rights." [19] The Sugar Act and Stamp Act of 1765 came at an inopportune time. The people were still emerging from postwar depression. As author Robert J. Taylor acknowledges, "money was scarce, trade was stagnant, and land values were sinking." [20] George Grenville, Chancellor of the Exchequer, sought to secure revenue for Great Britain for it to run its empire, which became an economic threat for the colonists.

The Stamp Act of 1765 had a direct effect on men of influence, such as lawyers, merchants, tavern keepers, and printers. The upper ranks of society were affected by Parliament's taxation, which helped perpetuate the revolution. These men of influence used their positions to create upheaval within colonial society. This upheaval consisted of non-consumption and non-importation. Connecticut, like other colonies, did not want to see their rights infringed upon, which gradually caused separation from the empire. Connecticut was a highly self-interested colony that supported American liberty, but never took more than a verbal stand until the news of bloodshed in Lexington and Concord.

There were various methods Connecticut used to prove its seriousness within the war effort. Although Connecticut enjoyed more liberties than other colonies they began calling up its militia to provide defense for their colony as a precaution. Connecticut urged its ministers to preach unity to their congregations and to guide their leaders as they sought to protect their liberties. The colony offered bounties for rifles, gun-locks, sulfur, and saltpeter that were locally manufactured. People soon realized that British supremacy and American liberty were "not compatible with each other." [21] The people of Connecticut appeared to be both, economically and ideologically motivated to join the war effort. Their reluctance to join only proved why Martin, his parents, and grandparents were all under the assumption that independence was their natural right. Connecticut's leaders had viewed their colony as independent and free. It would take Parliamentary taxation and desertions of superiority for them to realize that their standard of living had dissolved.

Martin was fortunate to have grandparents who were wealthy and able to provide the stability he needed at such a young age. When he was a young boy, he remembered how the Stamp Act caused problems within the country, but at the time he did not understand the magnitude of it. It was not until he was around 13 or 14 when he began understanding the movement after the repeal of the Stamp Act and the destruction of the tea in Boston. His grandfather, whom he was close to, explained the "French War" and piqued his curiosity. Intrigued by the stories Martin's youthful zeal began to stir, but his grandfather was reluctant to give consent for Martin to join the war. Martin was reluctant to go to war and stated, "I am well, so I'll keep." He felt cowardly, but did not want to take his "carcass where bullets fly." [22] His knowledge of war was limited, but he remained open-minded to the possibility. When he heard the rumors that the British were spreading desolation and death along their route from Boston he became paranoid and frightened.

By 1774, Martin realized that the potential for war was growing each and every day, but was determined not to become a part of it. Martin was busily employed at his grandparents farm and lived a fortunate lifestyle, which he later realized he should have never left, but stated that children are "full of notions." [23] Farming in Connecticut was difficult by any standard. "The work day," contends Robert J. Taylor, "was from sun-up to sun-down, or approximately fourteen hours, during the growing season, six days a week." [24] Hard work was necessary every day of the year, but somehow the colonists found time for recreational activities.

His grandfather gave him "play days" where he could fish, go gunning, or any other type of recreational activity. Fishing was considered one of the main staples of recreation. The plentiful population of shad and salmon enabled the colonists to have an excuse for "merrymaking and feasting." [25] Despite the standard of living in Connecticut, the notions of gaining money and feeling cowardly while many of Martin's "young associates" were joining the war gave him reason to be proactive. [26] Martin then decided to sacrifice his youth for the good of the country.

The war was a frightening prospect for the young Martin who was only 15 years old in 1775. His grandparents had harbored some troops from Boston and New York. The troops enabled him to gain courage from their company and conversation. Martin's grandfather told him he would never give consent for him to join the army unless he had consent from his parents. As Martin's courage grew, so did his desire to be called a soldier, and he began forming plans to get consent to join. When war began in 1775, he started understanding the differences between "this country" and "the mother country." [27] He found himself to no longer be frightened and called himself as "warm a patriot" as the best of them. [28]

Throughout Martin's childhood, he appeared to have plenty of opportunities to alienate himself from the war in order to ensure his survival. However, Martin developed a passion to serve his country as he believed Americans were "invincible." [29] He was leaving behind his youthful days in which he could have acquired an education or learned a trade. Instead, Martin decided to put his life in danger by defending his country. The standard of living for Martin offered many possibilities for his life, but he made the conscious decision to subject himself to the revolutionary cause. Despite having a good life at his grandparents, he was never taught grammar and was only able to acquire knowledge of the rules and articles of war. Martin's early life presented many opportunities for him to achieve elevated status within society. Instead, he chose to fight for the revolutionary cause from the lowest rank: a private soldier.

Another revolutionary born the same year (1760) as Martin was John Greenwood. He was born in Boston, Massachusetts on May 17, 1760, but moved to Maine at the age of 13 to live with his father's only brother who was a wealthy man. Before he relocated to Maine, he was able to acquire a limited education. He was educated in the North School where he did not learn grammar or spelling. According to Greenwood, there were two masters who had the arduous task of overlooking 300 to 400 boys. Greenwood mentioned that "all that we learned was acquired by the mere dint of having it thumped in," as the two masters could afford them little attention. [30] Therefore, he was not taught anything of significance while attending school.

The war was beginning to take shape while Greenwood was in school. He had heard many stories from the young boys which pointed to the war being imminent. Many of the boys eventually came to the conclusion that these events must come in the course of nature. Greenwood, on the other hand, became dismayed by the rumors. "For my part," Greenwood recollected, "all I wished was that church which stood by the side of my father's garden would fall on me at the time these terrible things happened, and crush me to death at once, so as to be out of pain quick." [31] Like Martin, it would take time for Greenwood to develop the courage and ardor necessary to become a revolutionary.

Opportunities, such as a trade or apprenticeship were limited for Greenwood, especially since he was only 15 years old when the war began. He was forced to leave behind a good opportunity with his uncle who could have provided him with an education. He also left the relative safety of Maine and put himself in a dangerous situation at an early age. The war had claimed his youthful days, and made it difficult for him to pursue a trade. Socially, it was difficult for Greenwood to not perceive himself as a coward. Before the revolution began, the rumors of war had caused great confusion for Greenwood with his future being insecure.

Boston also produced another ordinary man, who did not come from a wealthy family. His name was George Robert Twelves Hewes, born on August 25, 1742, in Boston, Massachusetts. [32] Hewes was the sixth out of nine children and was the son of a poor tanner and chandler. [33] Despite not being from a well-to-do family, his parents were able to afford early schooling for him. [34] In 1756, at the age of 14, Hewes was able to procure an apprenticeship as a shoemaker. [35] The Hewes family had limited connections in Boston, which was required for obtaining a good trade. George became a shoemaker because that seemed to be the only opportunity for him.

In 1763, after being denied his enlistment by the British army for being too short, he was able to open his own shoemaking shop. During the colonial period, shoemaking was not an ideal trade and Hewes was constantly looking for a way to escape this trade. The military provided an opportunity for what Hewes called his "depressed condition" as a shoemaker. [36] In the late 1760s, Hewes ended up in debtors' jail for not being financially able to pay his debt. [37] Hewes was clearly seeking more from life and he had "resolved to engage in the military service of my country, should an opportunity present." [38] Coming from a depressed condition, Hewes was forced to work up the social ladder.

Another ordinary New England man facing insecurity was Jeremiah Greenman. He was born in Newport, Rhode Island on May 7, 1758. Greenman's family came from "a long line of plain people." [39] His family seemed to have appeared in Massachusetts in the middle of the seventeenth century. The only source to list his family's arrival is a family Bible register page. One name on the list was "Wm Greenman," who was born "at Plimoth Mass" in 1652. [40] William Greenman settled in Swansea, Massachusetts in the early eighteenth century, when he soon became married and began to raise a family. Jeremiah's father, Jeremiah senior, was born on February 11, 1719/20. When Jeremiah senior became of age, he moved to Newport, Rhode Island. In 1749, he married Amy Wiles. It is not known why he moved, but one can only imagine that he was attracted to the maritime industry that was thriving in Newport.

In Newport, Jeremiah was able to receive "in his native town such an education as the Common Schools afforded." [41] This education was more or less elementary because Rhode Island had limited free public education for its children compared to the rest of New England. Newport was mainly comprised of tuition schools with limited free education for poor children. Greenman learned how to write during the war, not in the common school.

A prominent officer, General William Barton, was also born in Rhode Island. Barton was born in the small village of Warren on May 26, 1748. Warren was on the east side of the Narragansett Bay and nearly twenty miles from Newport, the birthplace of Jeremiah Greenman. Barton's father, Benjamin, was considered "an honest and respectable man." [42] Barton had the luxury of obtaining a common school education, which enabled him to acquire a trade when he became of age.

Once he served his apprenticeship, he became a shop owner dealing in the hatter's business. By the age of 22, he was united in marriage to Rhoda Carver, the daughter of Joseph Carver, of Bridgewater, Massachusetts. By 1773, the young couple quickly produced two children. Life for Barton was comfortable and pleasant with his business doing well. When Great Britain began to influence Rhode Island, he grew deep feelings of resentment. However, Barton had a family to console, which prevented him from joining the revolutionaries. The Battle of Bunker Hill ignited Barton's decision to join the American forces. Many people in Rhode Island feared that if Boston succumbed to the British, Providence would be the next target of attack.

On June 19, 1775, Barton offered his service as a volunteer in Boston. Bunker Hill was fought two days earlier and the British would not evacuate Boston until March 1776. Barton then decided to join the army and sacrifice himself for his country. He gave control of his business to a Mr. Lathrop and entered the army as a corporal. He rapidly ascended through the ranks before earning the promotion of Captain. As he fought the British, he became knowledgeable on military tactics. His work under the command of George Washington enabled him to pick up on the nuances of danger, military discipline, and cleanliness within the military.

While in Boston, Barton began to hear rumors of the British taking over Rhode Island. Threatening messages, such as "the town would be burnt at such as hour next day" were consistently being directed towards Newport. Newport did not have the means to resist the enemy as the people were considered to be "peaceable and unarmed inhabitants." [43] England had not yet regarded Rhode Island as traitorous and was "seeking by every means to conciliate her rebellious subjects." [44] Those "paternal chastisements" only created more dissension for Rhode Island since they were seeking full independence.

The indignant Barton returned home to Providence to settle his business and made arrangements to protect his family. Afterwards, he intended to return to the army, but Newport needed protection. Barton received orders to take his men to Tiverton, Rhode Island to create a defense. The people of Newport praised Barton for his "social qualities, his politeness, constant good humor, and patriotic sentiments." [45] Barton appeared to be a well-respected and distinguished man within his community.

Another Rhode Islander was Stephen Olney who became an officer in the Continental Army. Olney was born in the town of North Providence (*Colony*, as it was then called) on September 17, 1756. The farm in which he was born made him the fifth generation to occupy the same land. It was the first settlement of the state that was purchased by Thomas Olney who was a joint proprietor in the "Providence Purchase." [46] The Olney family believed in Puritanical views. Stephen Olney intended to spend his life "in the peaceful pursuits of agriculture; having no wishes beyond the boundaries of his farm, in plenty and rural quiet; the sound of war, and indeed of contention of any kind had never disturbed his habitation." [47] The war presented a life-altering change for Olney.

At the age of 20, he married and planned to cultivate his farm with a family of his own. His dream was to follow in his father's footsteps and to live in relative obscurity. When war seemed inevitable, Olney felt compelled to serve his country. In 1774, he joined a chartered military company called the North-Providence Rangers as a private. The object of the North-Providence Rangers was "to learn military tactics, and to be prepared to act in defence of our country's rights." [48] Olney joined under the belief that British advancement had threatened the freedom of his family. Many colonists felt that the British intended to enslave them without having independence. With the revolution imminent, Olney decided to fight for his country.

By May 1775, Olney wrote that "Rhode Island ordered three regiments to be raised for the protection of the colony." Olney stated he "was honored with an Ensign's commission in Captain John Angell's company, second Rhode-Island regiment, commanded by Colonel Hitchcock." Olney was a modest man and was unsure of how he obtained the commission. He reached the conclusion that Rhode Island could get no better men than himself. Although he accepted his commission, Olney wrote he did so "with much diffidence as to my qualifications; my education was but common for that day, and worst of all, what I had learned was mostly wrong." [49] Despite having a limited education, he was able to secure a commission from the military.

The circumstances in Rhode Island were different from those in Massachusetts. Rhode Island was a colony that enjoyed relative autonomy from Great Britain, similar to Connecticut, but, unlike Massachusetts. Olney wrote that "many (in Rhode Island) were deterred from embarking in the cause for fear they might be hanged up for rebels by order of our then gracious sovereign, George III." [50] Massachusetts had an abundance of men who sought to protect their rights. Rhode Island would eventually be forced to defend their fights.

Colonial Rhode Island was largely isolated from the rest of the colonies, freeing them to make their own decisions. Rhode Island towns "were all founded so that their inhabitants would not have to live with other people." [51] They were living an independent lifestyle compared to the inhabitants of Massachusetts. The people were also able to practice their own religious beliefs, since they were mostly considered outcasts from other colonies. Sydney James also noted that Rhode Island was able to deal with the royal government as a "fairy tale court." [52] British politics heavily influenced Rhode Islanders who viewed their colony as being a province in the British Empire.

Rhode Islanders enjoyed prosperity in trade, agricultural expansion, and unfamiliar religions. Providence and Newport became the commercial centers for Rhode Island. Providence constantly challenged the dominance of Newport commerce, which inspired an increase in population in the eighteenth century. Most of Rhode Island's population consisted of "farm families living on a simple scale and practicing many trades part-time in a rudimentary way." [53] Barton and Olney proved that there was opportunity in Rhode Island.

The colony consisted of wealthy merchants, military heroes, shopkeepers, full-time artisans, and leisured dilettantes. During the eighteenth century, Rhode Island was a peculiar colony, but offered a variety of opportunities, even for those of the lower class. Few Newport men attended college, but did have a limited education that often sufficed when finding employment. Many in Rhode Island lived with low or virtually nonexistent taxes and any type of agricultural product could achieve a good price. For most of rural Rhode Island, it was a land of small farms that produced livestock and small amounts of grain or dairy products for market. Most men were yeoman farmers who worked according to the seasons. Olney envisioned living this type of modest lifestyle.

Like every colonial town, Rhode Island had its share of disparity in wealth. There were paupers, poverty and limited opportunity to advance in society. There were also wealthy men who owned large estates. According to Sydney James, however, the most common of people was "an assortment of go-getters." [54] These men enabled Rhode Island to thrive under its semi-autonomous position in the British Empire. However, on the eve of the Revolution, Rhode Island was forced to change its peaceable and autonomous lifestyle. Britain had increased its power within the colonies, particularly in New England.

North of Rhode Island was Massachusetts, the apex of the war effort, which produced numerous high ranking members for inclusion in the war. One of these high ranking members was Benjamin Gilbert. He was born on May 31, 1755 in Brookfield, Massachusetts. [55] His father, Daniel, was a selectman who served in the French Wars of the 1740s and 1750s. Daniel would eventually serve as an officer under the distinctions of ensign, lieutenant, and captain. Benjamin's uncle, Joseph, was also a captain of a minuteman group. [56] The military served a large role in the Gilbert family.

Benjamin Gilbert was the eldest child and attended school in Brookfield, but beyond that he was self-taught, and self-made. Brookfield would play an aggressive role in the revolution and helped influence Gilbert's decision to become involved in the military. Brookfield opposed the tea taxes and supported the non-importation and non-consumption agreements. Anyone that imported and/or consumed the tea would be "held in utmost contempt, and be deemed enemies to the well-being of this country." [57] Gilbert's birth date, family expectations, a limited education, and the threat of the British all contributed to his decision to join the war. At nineteen years old, the army was the only opportunity for Gilbert when he enlisted in 1775 as a "fifer" in a

Brookfield company of minutemen. [58] For Gilbert, the war came at an inopportune moment in his life.

Another member of the upper class was Benjamin Tallmadge. He was from a wealthy family in Long Island, New York. Though New York was not considered New England, author Charles Swain Hall eloquently states "its environment was largely conditioned by Puritan institutions." [59] Since 1655, New England settlers were migrating to western Long Island, in particular the town of Setauket. This town was provincially governed by New York, but as Swain states "its inhabitants clung tenaciously to the independent New England form of local supervision – the town meeting." [60] Long Island also enjoyed coastal trading with New England and closer relations with Connecticut than with New York. Hence, Long Island resembled a New England colony. Tallmadge seems to identify more closely with a New Englander than a New Yorker.

In 1752, Benjamin's father was hired to be a minister for the Congregational Church of Setauket, Long Island. His father graduated from Yale College in 1747 and taught in the Hopkins Grammar School in New Haven, Connecticut before switching to ministry. In 1750, he married Susanna Smith, the daughter of John Smith, who was a minister for the White Plains Congregational Church. Benjamin continued ministry for 41 years before retiring. Although Benjamin and Susanna were originally from Connecticut, their five children grew up in Setauket. Their second son, Benjamin, was born on February 25, 1754. His father had the luxury of "preparing a number of boys (five sons) for college" and believed Benjamin was the best suited for college. [61]

Benjamin was deemed eligible for college at 12 or 13 years old, but his father said it was improper because he was so young. By 1769, he was admitted into Yale College where he could obtain a liberal education. At the time, according to Swain, the tuition for Yale College was twelve shillings. It was an education that most could not afford and left many ordinary men constantly deferring to educated men, such as Tallmadge.

At Yale College, Tallmadge became fluent in Latin and Greek, and studied natural philosophy, astronomy, mathematics, and metaphysics. There were also courses on logic and rhetoric, but mostly subjects involved training for the ministry. By 1773, when Tallmadge graduated, he was considered a promising young leader with opportunities to succeed. Tallmadge received "an application to superintend the High School in Weathersfield." He accepted the offer and stated he was "very much gratified and pleased, both with my employment and the people." [62] The socioeconomic status of Tallmadge's family helped contribute to his high position in society.

The Battle of Lexington - one of the first military engagements of the American Revolution - "electrified" the whole country. Tallmadge traveled to Boston where he met an acquaintance, Captain Chester, who had served at Bunker Hill. Chester offered Tallmadge the prospect of joining the army, but the military was not a priority for him. However, after much contemplation, Tallmadge believed he was influenced by the most patriotic principles and decided to accept Chester's offer. Tallmadge stated that he was "full of zeal in the cause of my country." [63] His father, a Whig of Revolution, believed Tallmadge had opportunity outside of the military and was reluctant to give him consent. Despite his father's reluctance, Tallmadge joined and his father was surprised to see his son wearing a military uniform. Tallmadge appeared to be motivated by patriotism, but also by the prospect of social, economic, and political incentive.

Olney and Barton, both officers from Rhode Island, joined the war because they sought to defend their country. On the other hand, Gilbert and Tallmadge, both officers from Massachusetts, joined the war to obtain military commissions and to promote their own self-interests. Each colony was faced with different circumstances that motivated the colonists - lower and upper class - to join the American Revolution.

[17] Joseph Plumb Martin, *A Narrative of a Revolutionary Soldier: Some of the Adventures, Dangers, and Sufferings of Joseph Plumb Martin* (New York: Signet Classic, 2001), 5.

[18] Robert J. Taylor, *Colonial Connecticut: A History* (New York: KTO Press, 1979), 101.

[19] Ibid., 246.

[20] Ibid., 221.

[21] Ibid., 239.

[22] Martin, *A Narrative of a Revolutionary Soldier*, 7.

[23] Ibid., 6.

[24] Taylor, *Colonial Connecticut*, 180-181.

[25] Ibid., 182.

[26] Martin, *A Narrative of a Revolutionary Soldier*, 9.

[27] Ibid., 12.

[28] Ibid. 15.

[29] Ibid., 16.

[30] John Greenwood, *The Wartime Services of John Greenwood: A Young Patriot in the American Revolution, 1775-1783* (Tyrone, Pa: Westvaco, 1981), 39.

[31] Ibid., 40.

[32] Alfred F. Young. *The Shoemaker and the Tea Party*, Boston, Massachusetts: Beacon Press, 1999, 11.

[33] Ibid., 11-12.

[34] Ibid., 12.

[35] Ibid., 12-13.

[36] Ibid., 17.

[37] Ibid., 22.

[38] Ibid., 17.

[39] Jeremiah Greenman, *Diary of a Common Soldier in the American Revolution, 1775-1783: an Annotated Edition of the Military Journal of Jeremiah Greenman* (DeKalb: Northern Illinois University Press, 1978), xiii.

[40] Ibid., xiii.

[41] Ibid., xiv.

[42] Catharine R. Williams, *Biography of Revolutionary Heroes; Containing the Life of Brigadier Gen. William Barton, and also, of Captain Stephen Olney* (New York: Wiley & Putnam, 1839), 27.

[43] Ibid., 30.

[44] Ibid., 31.

[45] Ibid., 32.

[46] Ibid., 145.

[47] Ibid., 148.

[48] Ibid., 150.

[49] Ibid.

[50] Ibid.

[51] Sydney V. James, *Colonial Rhode Island: a History* (New York: Charles Scribner's Sons, 1975), 13.

[52] Ibid., 229.

[53] Ibid., 232.

[54] Ibid., 259.

[55] John Shy. *Winding Down: the Revolutionary War letters of Lieutenant Benjamin Gilbert of Massachusetts, 1780-1783: from his original manuscript letterbook* (Ann Arbor: University of Michigan Press, 1989), 109.

[56] Ibid., 11.

[57] Ibid., 12.

[58] Ibid., 11.

[59] Charles Swain Hall, *Benjamin Tallmadge: Revolutionary Soldier and American Businessman* (New York: AMS Press, 1966), 3.

[60] Ibid., 4.

[61] Ibid., 3.

[62] Benjamin Tallmadge, *Memoir of Col. Benjamin Tallmadge* (New York: Arno Press, 1968), 6.

[63] Ibid., 7.

Chapter 2

Revolution: Private Soldiers and Their Motivations

Before the revolution, poverty in parts of New England was increasing as opportunities were dwindling. The revolution came at an opportune time for many lower class individuals as they sought a better life. These lower class men did not have the same security and options as the upper class. However, it would be up to these men to join the army in order for America to succeed against British advancement. Private soldiers, or lower class men, were motivated by social, economic, and political factors. The army would afford them little opportunity, but they would prove their worth during the war.

Tensions rose when the destruction of the tea occurred in Boston. By 1773, there was a devotion to nothing but war, liberty, or death. The first year of the war marked a time period when colonists were becoming involved in the military service to display their patriotism. It was, as Charles Royster notes, a "rage militaire." [64] Ordinary people wanted to contribute to their country's cause with pride being a major factor. By 1776, the military decided to raise a more distinct group of soldiers.

The number of ardent volunteers for regular military services began to decrease when many colonists expected an economic incentive for their services. The war became an opportunity for youths who wanted to become gentlemen. After the first year, Royster contends that the "army's survival, discipline, and patriotism helped to sustain the revolutionaries' perseverance." [65] There appeared to be less patriotism, however, as the war progressed. American soldiers were encouraged by the battles they had won, but recruiting and enlistments became a constant struggle for officers and Congress. It would take an economic incentive to increase the number of men to display their patriotism. Congress was forced to make ill-advised promises to entice men into the military. Individuals were not willing to sacrifice their lives until they were offered economic security.

Defending their country in its time of need was significant to the men, but was not their only motive for joining the war effort. As historian Charles Knowles Bolton suggests, "these men had clung to army life for its few bright spots, but also its many days of privation." [66] This statement showed they were willing to subject themselves through various hardships and privations while also securing freedom for America. Without the lower class in New England facing limited opportunity and poverty, then America may not have succeeded in the war effort. It was men, such as Joseph Plumb Martin, George Robert Twelves Hewes, John Greenwood, and Jeremiah Greenman who forced the issue and proved they were valuable commodities to America.

These men, along with many others, would go on to endure numerous hardships and privations with their future being undetermined. As William Huntting Howell suggests, these men would "starve to death in the service of a nation that does not yet exist." [67] Although Martin's life before the revolution was not one of narrowing opportunity and poverty, he enlisted in the army as a private soldier. A private soldier was the lowest rank. They put their lives in danger without adequate resources to combat the enemy. Martin saw value in fighting for his country and felt the country deserved its liberty. His life before the revolution was comfortable and secure, which showed that other motivational factors played a role in his decision to join.

For Martin, joining the war effort was enhanced by the potential economic incentive offered by the Continental Congress. For colonists who had no other prospects and limited education, the war offered social and economic opportunities. Martin began to show immediate support for the revolutionary cause when he learned that Congress would offer one dollar to any private soldier willing to join the military ranks. Charles Royster noted that on September 6, 1776, "Congress offered twenty dollars and one hundred acres of land to men who enlisted for the duration." [68] Martin enlisted for six months, instead of the duration of the war, because he wanted to grasp the complexities of war. Listening to his grandfather's stories of war gave Martin a sense of fear. War meant he would often have to deal with starvation, fatigue, and survival. Martin felt it was best to enlist for a short period of time rather than committing himself for the duration.

It was widely rumored that "many Americans feared that by long and indefinite enlistments they would lose their freedom." [69] Perhaps, Martin also feared enslavement by the British if the Americans were defeated. The enlisted men expected and wanted to be paid for their service. For many soldiers, fighting for one's country became perilous without having confidence in a secure future. Many individuals were forced to grapple with the idea of fighting for the country.

The colonies quickly realized that if no bounty was offered then their regiments would not be full. Royster suggested that "bounties inspired some soldiers to enlist several times with several units within a few days." [70] It was a bold attempt to gather soldiers as volunteers and many men needed to work to fulfill their obligations at home. By June 26, 1776, Congress voted "to grant ten dollars to men who enlisted for three years." [71] Congress had hoped to inspire the men with incentives to serve their country. Patriotism, while noble, also came at a price.

During the war, soldiers began to realize how bad the situation was in America. The government had few resources, including money and food to compensate the soldiers for their efforts. Private soldiers became aggravated because they felt their efforts were not appreciated. The officers, however, had more advantages and suffered less. The private soldiers became motivated by the suffering and lack of respect they received.

Pride became a major underlying factor towards gaining independence. The private soldiers were resilient and constantly sought to prove themselves, despite the lack of support. Desertion was viewed as a disgraceful act, but many intended to maintain their self-respect and pride. Being considered a coward would be harmful to their reputation. Under this reasoning many decided it was better to endure hardships and deprivation rather than disgrace themselves and their country. There was an understanding that if they lost the war, the British would induce far greater consequences upon them than their own government did during the war. In short, the ill-advised promises made by Congress had inspired the revolutionaries to gain independence.

From the beginning of the war, political motives became commonplace among both, the upper and lower classes. The private soldiers used politics to their advantage during their battle for survival. Congress was forced to economically persuade these men because many felt an incentive was needed to join the war effort. If the soldiers were going to endure privation throughout the war, Congress needed to make their experience worthwhile. Facing limited resources, including food, clothing, blankets, tents, and arms the private soldiers sought to prove they were equal to the officers. During the war, many private soldiers used their suffering as a political weapon to show they would not falter under harrowing circumstances.

During the winter of 1775-1776, Martin felt as anxious as ever to defend his country, especially since he gathered the full understanding of war. Martin, at his young age, believed the Americans were "invincible," which showed his youthful side. [72] The suffering was just beginning for Martin and his fellow soldiers as the search for food increased daily.

The "Kip's Bay Affair" became a vulnerable spot for the American troops. [73] Not only were Martin and his comrades forced to fight off a British attack, but Martin needed to help his sick friend who was overcome by heat, fatigue, and hunger. At one point, he was forced to leave his friend for a short time to help fight off the British. He had to conceal himself in the bushes and weeds in order to survive. He stated the British were so close that he "could see the buttons on their clothes." [74] Once the British withdrew, he went back to his sick comrade where he realized he was sleep deprived and had not eaten in 24 hours, but still managed to get his friend help. One officer showed little compassion and told Martin, "well, if he dies the country will be rid of one who can do it no good." [75] That was an unforgettable statement, which angered Martin and showed the differences between the highest and lowest ranks.

The next day the colonists found themselves fighting the British again, but this time was different. The men were fatigued and suffered with hunger for 48 hours. One soldier complained of being hungry next to the Lieutenant Colonel. He gave the soldier a burnt piece of Indian corn and told him to "eat this and learn how to be a soldier." [76] Martin was rapidly learning how to be a soldier and it was a humbling experience for him. After the battle, the men went back to camp where they were able to eat a meal. Even this was not a pleasant experience for Martin, but he had no choice - he was starving. They ate beef that was burnt "as black as a coal" on the outside and raw on the inside. [77] Martin describes the men as not having anything to eat for "forty-eight hours," which caused much fatigue and faintness. [78] The private soldiers were often deprived of the necessities, but when they were offered food, they did not complain. Martin recollected that a wise man said "a full belly loatheth a honeycomb: but to the hungry soul every bitter thing is sweet." [79] Starvation eventually became a secondary matter because they also had to face hard duty and near nakedness in cold weather.

The private soldiers had lost all their clothes in the "Kip's Bay Affair" and were not adequately supplied. That meant they would be forced to sleep on the cold, and often wet, ground with no blankets. Dealing with starvation became a daily occurrence within the Continental Army for most. Martin would attempt to find anything possible to put in his stomach. He would forage in the woods to take advantage of nature's offerings, such as chestnuts and animals.

At the beginning of the war, Martin was reluctant to ask for food, but he soon began stealing and gathering as much as he could. It was widely known that America was a poor country at the time so it became survival of the fittest for the soldiers and even the officers, who fared better than the soldiers. Those first six months taught him that "Uncle Sam" was more than willing to provide arms and ammunition for the troops, but never enough to eat, drink, or wear. [80]

When Thanksgiving arrived in 1777, Congress announced they wanted the army to celebrate the occasion and to close out the "year of high living." [81] For all their previous sufferings, each man was awarded a gill of rice and a tablespoon of vinegar. The army was demoralized and angry by the failed promises because they felt they had been awarded virtually nothing for defending their country. Most men had to march barefoot over rough and frozen terrain which caused their feet to be frostbitten. Congress did not make their jobs any easier, often making it worse for the soldiers.

The misfortunes of the private soldiers quickly spread throughout the colonies and made others reluctant to enlist. One of the greatest misfortunes throughout the war was not being adequately supplied. Many of the private soldiers were being ruled unfit for service due to illnesses from the harsh weather conditions. Approximately 2,000 men were ruled unfit for duty in November 1777 and by December that number rose to 2,898. [82] Nearly 3,000 men in 1777 could not defend their country because they mainly lacked shoes or shirts. With limited provisions, this not only created bad morale, but also the efficiency of the army decreased dramatically.

The men were true patriots, that can never be questioned, but they had suffered for four long years. Martin and others constantly complained to the officers and showed their dissatisfaction, but it was to no avail. During the campaign of 1780, stationed around Westfield, New Jersey, the private soldiers organized a mutiny after the officers failed to listen to their complaints. Each regiment unified, disobeying all orders, and took up arms against the officers. The mutiny was successful and the men did obtain better provisions. The private soldiers were too prideful to desert the army because that would be deserting the country.

On December 25, 1776, Martin was honorably discharged from the army after serving his enlistment time. It was now his decision to re-enlist or begin a new life outside of the war. Martin suggested "the general opinion of the people was, that the war would not continue three years longer; what reasons they had for making such conjectures I cannot imagine." [83] He was being recruited heavily to rejoin the war effort, but after suffering throughout the war, he had no desire to return. Men were enlisting as soon as the weather turned warm again, which made his decision even more difficult.

His "most familiar associate" enlisted for the duration of the war as a sergeant. [84] That man constantly pressured Martin to rejoin the war effort. Martin mentioned how "that little insignificant monosyllable-No-was the hardest word in the language for me to pronounce." [85] Martin was heavily influenced by his friends joining the army and could not be thought a coward for not rejoining. Martin made the decision to join again at the urging of his friend, but soon realized he made the wrong choice. At that point, he "began sorely to repent" his decision. [86] He requested permission to be relieved of duty. The Captain granted his request and Martin would only join again on his terms.

Martin wanted to join a dignified squad when the opportunity arose. He had an "elbow relation, a sort of cousin-in-law" who had obtained a Lieutenants commission. His cousin-in-law had constantly urged his grandparents to give their consent for Martin to join him in his squad. He eventually obtained consent to rejoin the army. The squad offered him a position and Martin thought he "might as well endeavour to get as much for my skin as I could." [87] He had rejoined the army, and once again his primary motivation appeared to be economic incentive. He stated "the men gave me what they agreed to, I forget the sum, perhaps enough to keep the blood circulating." [88] Martin was well-aware of the dangers and suffering he would again face, but in order for him to join he made sure to procure a financial settlement.

In 1780, Martin was transferred to the Sappers and Miners regiment, where he was promoted to sergeant. For four years, the men "absolutely, literally starved" and the suffering "tried men's souls." [89] His suffering did not go unrecognized by his Lieutenant while they were at Newburgh obtaining provisions for the army. The Lieutenant hinted that Martin should pick out the better articles of clothing from the provisions. Other sergeants did not understand Martin's need for clothing, but the Lieutenant quickly intervened and told the men that he deserved it for suffering through much of the war while they were in the safety of their homes. As the war progressed, Martin learned not to be bashful and took advantage of every opportunity to further his survival.

The campaign of 1782 occurred when Martin, along with numerous others, were diagnosed with yellow fever. Martin suffered an attack of it in February and struggled greatly until March. It caused him to bleed profusely from his nose, and his body strength was reduced substantially within the first few days. Martin said he was "as helpless as an infant." [90] The officers were forced to build a room for a hospital where Martin was transferred to recover. During his stay in the hospital, he watched people die from diseases. As much as he suffered from his previous war encounters, this became a nearly unbearable experience as he prepared himself for death. He would go on to survive the disease, but that experience put the war in perspective. For Martin, the American army soon became the enemy as they helped perpetuate his near death experience by not providing adequate supplies. Martin and his comrades would go on to suffer until the end of the war in 1783.

One of the biggest obstacles was supply. The country was young and poor, which made it difficult for them to supply shoes, clothing, food, firearms, ammunition, tents, and cooking equipment. For the most part, these items had to be found on a massive scale. The French were able to provide substantial help, especially after Louis XVI signed the Treaty of Amity and Commerce in February of 1778. The French provided much needed help, but the supplies had to come mainly from the Americans. Several reasons contributed to the lack of supply. The enthusiasm for the war waned greatly in 1777 through 1779. Another reason was American farmers and artisans were producing goods for all three armies (Americans, British, and the French) in order to profit. The third reason is the two foreign armies could pay in hard coin, gold and silver, which the Americans lacked. Finally, the demands of the army and the British blockade created shortages of meat, grain, salt, clothes, shoes, gunpowder, and imported goods, such as tea, spices, and rum. The private soldiers had to deal with these shortages on a daily basis. They were forced to adapt to starvation and coldness in order to ensure their survival.

Before the revolution, Martin acknowledged patriotism, personal sacrifice, bravery, and confidence in winning the war, but those items began to fade as the war continued. He was intrigued by various war stories, adventure, and most of all the money offered for enlisted men. From his perspective, he had already acknowledged that America was its own country and they were fighting against "the mother country." [91] He dispels the typical military glory and heroism often told by the upper class. He was adamant that war should not be glorified. Martin and his comrades joined the war for various reasons, but nationalism became an afterthought as many soldiers suffered throughout the war. He describes America as being "young and poor," but was still able to triumph over a far superior enemy. [92]

Martin's revolution was no different than most other private soldiers. George Robert Twelves Hewes saw the revolution as an opportunity for advancement in society. He repudiated deference within society and believed no man should be subjected to social classes. The Revolution provided him and others with the opportunity to enhance their status in society. Hewes and Martin were similar as both men were ideologically independent before the war occurred.

Hewes and Martin, as private soldiers, sought to use the revolution to prove their worth in a society that generally overlooked their abilities. The narrowing opportunities in Boston caused

Hewes to join the revolution as the war offered opportunity. He was an ordinary, poor citizen who relied on his honesty and zeal to make himself known to the elites of society.

Around 1770, Hewes became politically active when the Boston Massacre occurred. Hewes led a poverty-stricken life, but he earned a living as an artisan. Hewes became the epitome of how lower class individuals were "more likely to resort to collective actions to seek their goals." Poverty and limited opportunity forced Hewes into "political deference," or becoming dependent upon the upper class. In search of modest opportunity, many lower class individuals used collective action as a political weapon. Hewes, like many others, only wanted to have a voice in society without being dependent upon the upper class. They were not only fighting for independence against Britain, but also against the social hierarchy.

Hewes was willing to sacrifice his life in the revolutionary cause by declaring himself a patriot. However, other motives perpetuated his patriotism and national identity. Hewes' main motivational force for joining in the war effort was to enhance his social and economic standing. Inequality in society prevailed before the outbreak of war and Hewes, like other lower class individuals sought to destroy that notion. With the outbreak of war, Hewes and others took advantage by declaring themselves patriots in the cause for American independence. He wanted to create a national identity for the lower ranks of society. In short, it was his mission to gain a sense of citizenship and personal worth to denounce deference.

When Boston was put under martial law in 1775, he was forced to flee the city with his family. After sending his family to a safe location, his father's hometown of Wrentham, Massachusetts, Hewes was able to serve in the Boston militia and occasionally as a privateer for a few months out of the year. [93] He could only serve a limited amount of time during the war because he also had to provide for his family. [94] There can be no denying his ardent patriotism, but Hewes joined the war with notions of eliminating his poverty-stricken lifestyle by searching for such an opportunity.

The resistance movements of the Boston Massacre and the Boston Tea Party became events that would win Hewes recognition within the Boston community. Before the Revolution began, Hewes witnessed ordinary men being victimized by soldiers. The cruelty that was displayed by the British soldiers served as motivation for Hewes because he perceived the rights of the colonists were being trampled.

National identity for Hewes meant defending his "rights," actively supporting his countryman, and becoming a citizen within the American colonies. The personal experiences of Hewes left him "continually reflecting upon the unwarrantable sufferings inflicted on the citizens of Boston by the usurpation and tyranny of Great Britain, and my mind was excited with an unextingmshable desire to aid in chastising them." [95] Like many others, Hewes gained a sense of citizenship and personal worth through his traumatic war experiences. Hewes used the revolution to advance within society and to provide for his family.

Another soldier to take advantage of the war was John Greenwood. Greenwood's uncle lived in the town of Falmouth (Portland), Maine that was 150 miles from Boston. His uncle was a cabinet-maker and also dealt with the shipping business. Greenwood had an opportunity to learn a trade from his uncle, but the war intervened. His uncle was the lieutenant of an independent company called "the Cadets," where Greenwood was employed to play the fife while the company marched. [96] He was the only person in that area who knew how to play the fife and was treated favorably by the men.

Being thrown into a society of men who "imbibed the ardor of a military spirit" was difficult for Greenwood to comprehend, but he soon found the zeal to fight for his country. [97] His peers had garnished a strong sense of nationalism that had a profound effect on Greenwood. That nationalism gave him a sense of pride for his country. He continued to stay with his uncle until 1775 marking the beginning of the war. He returned to Boston since he feared his family may be killed by the British. Greenwood was cautious as he wanted to fight for his country, but naturally also feared he may be killed. He decided it was best to enlist for eight months to gain perspective on the operations of war. He also recalled that "to call it living was out of the question." [98] War had caused him to rethink his position in the military. He had lost the courage to fight because "everywhere the greatest terror and confusion seemed to prevail." [99]

He was frightened by the sheer chaos and terror that ensued between the Americans and the British. He developed the courage to fight when he stumbled upon a black man who was wounded in the neck. He asked the man if it hurt to which his response was "no" and he was only going to "get a plaster put on it," and planned to return. [100] The will of that man inspired Greenwood with immediate encouragement and pride for America. Fear never troubled him again as he felt brave, and like a soldier. Greenman did not gather a strong national identity until those personal experiences shaped his way of thinking.

Jeremiah Greenman, another revolutionary who enlisted as a private soldier, had different motivations for joining the war effort. Greenman served in the war for all eight years. At the time, Greenman felt the war occurred at an inopportune moment in his life. He was supposed to be preparing for a trade or career. There was little indication, however, that he actively pursued a trade or career. Therefore, the revolution may have occurred at the most opportune moment for Greenman.

Motivated by the lure of the military, which offered economic and social opportunity, he joined the army. The army offered the opportunity of patriotic service and also a livelihood. His service would be temporary and dangerous, but it gave him the opportunity "to make a man of himself." [101] He was motivated for several reasons, mainly social. He manipulated the military to gain a sense of perspective in his life. When the revolution began, he was only seventeen years old and decided the army would give him the most opportunity in life. He was willing to sacrifice his life while attempting to figure out his future endeavors. He also wanted to play a role in the birth of a nation.

---

[64] Royster, *A Revolutionary People*, 25.

[65] Ibid., 96-97.

[66] Charles Knowles Bolton, *The Private Soldier under Washington* (New York: Kennikat Press, 1902),

[67] William Huntting Howell, "Starving Memory: Joseph Plumb Martin Un-Tells the Story of the American Revolution," www.common-place.org 10, no. 2 (2010), http://www.common-place.org/vol-10/no-02/howell (accessed March 14, 2010)

[68] Royster, *A Revolutionary People at War*, 65.

[69] Ibid., 49.

[70] Ibid., 71-72.

[71] Ibid., 64.

[72] Martin, *A Narrative of a Revolutionary Soldier*, 16.

[73] Ibid., 30.

[74] Ibid., 33.

[75] Ibid., 35.

[76] Ibid., 38.

[77] Ibid., 39.

[78] Ibid., 38.

[79] Ibid., 59.

[80] Ibid., 55.

[81] Ibid., 87.

[82] Bolton, *The Private Soldier under Washington*, 100.

[83] Martin, *A Narrative of a Revolutionary Soldier*, 52.

[84] Ibid., 52.

[85] Ibid.

[86] Ibid., 53.

[87] Ibid.

[88] Ibid., 54.

[89] Ibid., 148.

[90] Ibid., 219.

[91] Ibid., 15.

[92] Ibid., 245.

[93] Young. *The Shoemaker and the Tea Party*, 52-53.

[94] Ibid.

[95] Ibid., 48.

[96] Greenwood, *The Wartime Services of John Greenwood*, 41.

[97] Ibid.

[98] Ibid., 46.

[99] Ibid., 49.

[100] Ibid.

[101] Greenman, *Diary of a Common Soldier*, xv.

Chapter Three

Revolution: Officers and Their Motivations

The Revolution for officers, as opposed to the private soldiers, presented a different type of opportunity. The officers viewed the Revolution as an opportunity to not only gain economic standing, but also social and political standing within society. Many officers came from wealthier families - giving them an option on whether or not they wanted to join the military and fight for their freedom. This chapter will focus on the following officers, Colonel Benjamin Tallmadge, Colonel William Barton, Captain Stephen Olney, and Lieutenant Benjamin Gilbert. Each of these men joined the American army for their own distinct reasons. However, one underlying theme emerges with these four men: they sought social and political greatness through the military. The motivational factors of why these four men decided to join the military will be examined in this chapter.

Colonel Benjamin Tallmadge proved to be full of zeal for his country, but he also viewed the pending revolution as an opportunity to present his qualities. When he first realized that war was inevitable, he was reluctant to join the war effort. It was not until he talked to Captain Chester that he realized the military offered an opportunity. Although Tallmadge had a strong sense of national identity, he was influenced by a desire to move up in the military ranks.

The beginning of the war, while in New York, he witnessed his first battle, which he described as "awful." [102] He also mentioned that he could hardly bring his mind "to be willing to attempt the life of a fellow-creature." [103] The campaign of 1776 marked a tumultuous period for Tallmadge as enlistments were expiring and recruits were decreasing with an enemy defeating them. Tallmadge also stated the enemy was "insolent and cruel both to the inhabitants and to their prisoners. In fact, all was confusion and dismay, and it seemed as if we were on the eve of despair and ruin." [104] Perhaps, the most glaring part of his commentary is that the enemy displayed cruelty towards the inhabitants and prisoners. It was this cruelty brought upon fellow Americans that gave them a sense of national identity. The cruel tactics displayed by the British had inadvertently inspired the revolutionaries with national pride and would protect America at all costs.

In the fall of 1776, Congress passed a quota to raise battalions of infantry in each state in the Union. They also authorized General George Washington to appoint officers for each regiment, which changed the military system. Tallmadge was among the appointed officers when he was offered "the first troop, in the 2d regiment of the light dragoons, commanded by Elisha Sheldon." He eventually enlisted the quota for his troops and obtained his "commission as captain bore date the 14th of December, 1776." Tallmadge had risen in the military ranks, while also serving his country. He was envisioning that this would be his "new career, both as to the nature and duration of my military service." By Tallmadge's estimation the dragoon service was "so honorable and so desireable, it became an object of primary importance to obtain an appointment in this corps." A common occurrence emerges throughout Tallmadge's account of the war: the Americans parlayed victories into hope. Tallmadge described the Battle of Trenton as being one "where gloom and dismay prevailed, zeal and courage began to appear." [105] The victory at Trenton inspired the troops to continue persevering, despite the enormous obstacle they faced with Great Britain.

The campaign of 1777 was described by Tallmadge as "my military duties by day, and the pleasant intercourse with the inhabitants in the evening, made the time pass rapidly away." [106] Tallmadge's motivational factors for his service were "military ambition" and "panting for glory." [107] Tallmadge appeared to envision himself as any other soldier, but needed to instill the motivation and hope into his troops. The officer's duty was to provide inspiration for his troops and Tallmadge seemed to excel at providing hope. On April 7, 1777, Tallmadge acquired the rank of Major in the 2nd Regiment Light Dragoons. He had earned his commission as a field officer.

During the war, Tallmadge and others received much needed motivation after being nearly decimated by the harsh winter at Valley Forge in 1778. The rumors of the French army, "about 6,000 strong, under the command of the Count Rochambeau," affording aid to the American cause became a realization that independence "of our country was absolutely sure." [108] They also expected a large fleet of reinforcements, too. Many soldiers believed the next campaign (1780) would be a decisive one for the American cause.

Another highly motivated officer, similar to Tallmadge, was Colonel William Barton. When the war began, Barton was stationed at Tiverton, Rhode Island. It was his military duty to protect the channel on the east side of Howland's ferry and to maintain correspondence with Newport, after the British came into possession. The British allowed them to depart with their families, but they were given only twenty four hours. The people of Newport had capitulated honorably, although the defenselessness and exposure only motivated the troops. Despite the capitulation, Barton had no sense of idleness as he was prepared to be more useful to his country.

Barton frequently contemplated ways in which to defeat the British. On several occasions he employed spies on the island to gather an exact location of the British in Newport. He had planned to surprise General Prescott, of the British army, in 1777. Barton was willing to go in alone as he prepared to "strike one blow for my country, if fate never permits me to strike another." [109] His determination was contagious among his troops who were motivated to strike the final blow to Great Britain.

Wartime experiences played an integral role in shaping the motivational factors in which the soldiers used to defeat the British. When the American forces saw their land decimated by foraging parties, it reinvigorated their passion to defend their country. Barton, like many officers and soldiers, viewed that as a lack of respect. He was determined to take only volunteers because they were "willing to risk their lives with him to advance two paces in front." [110] Barton viewed himself as an ordinary soldier as he pledged "to share every danger, whatever it might be, equally with his soldiers." [111] After contriving plans to surprise General Prescott, he eventually pursued that plan successfully. Barton had captured General Prescott, and although the British were stunned, their officers and privates "rejoiced to get rid of him" because he was "arbitrary and tyrannical," as well as "universally hated." [112] Barton witnessed the same atrocities the British wrought on the American prisoners as Tallmadge did. On February 22, 1777, Barton witnessed the harsh treatment the British were inflicting upon American prisoners. Captain John Lee, a fatal victim of the cruel treatment was one of seven men that Barton witnessed being brought to the hospital "in the most deplorable situation." [113] Barton also mentioned that many officers, privates, and negroes were confined within a vessel where "they were half starved, and denied even light for a number of days." [114] When the troops witnessed the cruelty, it provided extra motivation for them to succeed in defeating the British.

Although Barton perceived himself as being a common soldier and sharing equally with the privates, there were times when he took advantage of being an officer. He had the luxury of staying within quarters that were out of the elements, whereas privates were forced to camp on the ground in the most deplorable of conditions. Barton could also afford to secure a farm-house nearby where he housed his wife and children. Once he acquired his commission as Brevet

Colonel from Congress in the winter of 1777-1778, he was effectively removed from his

situation and was not immediately needed for actual military service. His troops were seemingly

demoralized by this situation as they respected Barton. Barton returned to Providence where he

had the fortunate opportunity of tending to his family affairs. Despite having time with his

family and working in his hatter's shop, he was interested in being called back to service for his

country.

When Barton's hometown of Warren had come into the possession of the British it

provided an opportunity for him to gather eager inhabitants to begin a militia. After he became

General of the Rhode-Island militia, along with Brevet Colonel in the United States Army,

Barton and his men arrived at Warren to find a retreating enemy. In the distance, they could hear

a large army making strides toward their position.

The author, Mrs. Williams, provided an anecdote that had been confirmed by Barton

himself. Barton had allegedly chased the enemy yelling "I am the man who took Prescott, and

by ---, if you will just step out of your lurking place, I'll hack you to pieces in less time than it

took to take him." [115] Barton chased the British to Bristol, where he was shot in his right thigh,

just above the knee, and lodged in his hip. Mrs. Williams mentioned the bullet was taken from

his hip and preserved by his family. She also mentioned that "a long and tedious illness was the

consequence of this wound. For three months the Colonel kept his bed. A lingering fever,

occasioned by his sufferings, set in, and for some time his life was in imminent danger." [116] His

character and devotion to the cause was never questioned.

While he recuperated, the enemy had threatened to possess the town. However, the Barton family was unable to relocate with a newborn child. Because of Barton's rank, General John Sullivan sent a message to not relocate as he would send a wagon to carry them to safety if they were in danger and that his family would be cared for first. [117] As a ranking officer, Barton was afforded the luxury of having the army take care of not only his family, but him as well. Private soldiers did not enjoy the luxury of seeing their families and they surely did not have offers to help save their families from an enemy threatening to invade their hometown.

Barton's return to the army was impeded by a long illness. It was with much regret that he could not return to duty with his fellow troops. However, he was appointed to sundry offices of honor and profit. He was also a member of the Legislature from Providence and the government appointed him to the office of inspector in the custom-house. Despite, carrying these various jobs, he was also a member of the Rhode Island House of Representatives. During the war, Barton's popularity had risen to the point of having a brig named after him called "William Barton." [118] Barton staunchly believed that America deserved its independence and he went to great lengths to see peace restored within the "bleeding country." [119] He was unable to participate in active duty, but he was still able to exert himself in the relief of the distressed inhabitants of captured towns, as well as those who had property destroyed. Barton had a prideful sense of nationalism and felt America was ready for independence from Great Britain.

Similar in character, was his Rhode Island comrade, Stephen Olney. Olney's primary motivation to join the war was his duty to country. He arose when his country needed him and was rewarded for his efforts. After joining the military in 1774, Olney wrote in his manuscript, that he sought "to learn military tactics, and to be prepared to act in defence of our country's rights." [120] It appears his motivation was based strongly on national identity and dedication to the cause. His devotion was quickly recognized as Olney stated "in May, 1775, the Colony of Rhode Island ordered three regiments to be raised for the protection of the Colony, and as part of an army of observation, and I, was honored with an Ensign's commission in Captain John Angell's company, second Rhode-Island regiment, commanded by Colonel Hitchcock." [121]

Just as Colonel William Barton, Stephen Olney displayed his modesty in his manuscript. In response to his Ensign's commission, he modestly states "who recommended me I do not know; but it was not by my own intercession. But perhaps they chose me because they could get no better, so many were deterred from embarking in the cause for fear they might be hanged up for rebels by order of our then gracious sovereign, George III." Despite being in dissent to his qualifications, he accepted his commission. Olney was the first to admit his education was "common for that day, and worst of all, what I had learned was mostly wrong." [122] It was clear, Olney was not expecting a commission, and he misconceived his own achievements. He was focused on understanding proper military tactics and strategy.

Olney envisioned the country defeating the British through sheer fortitude. The spirit of liberty had reached new heights and would be "reduced to hopeless and unconditional submission" before they would be defeated. [123] Olney admitted as they marched towards Roxbury and prepared for battle the regiments were in "high spirits, though with rather quivering apprehension, on first sight of the British." [124] Olney provided an anecdote of the war in his manuscript that displayed the difficulty of keeping the men motivated. "The Rhode-Island troops," wrote Olney, "were for some time drawn up just within reach of their shells, and not being acquainted with those sort of missiles, it was with great difficulty the men could be kept in the ranks, especially when they imagined a shell was about to light on their heads." [125] Olney animated the situation further by stating "fear always makes danger, and in order to prevent fear from warping my judgment, I held up my gun by the muzzle as a perpendicular, and kept my post, as did also our company." [126] He had successfully motivated his troops by leading by example in what seemed to be a chaotic situation.

The Americans used what motivation they could in order to keep spirits high within the ranks. As documented in numerous historical documents, the winters of 1775-1776 were brutal. Many soldiers suffered from cold and famine, but if the Americans suffered, then surely the British were suffering from the elements, too. The Americans used that suffering to motivate them as they understood the British had a large number of their wounded die from fatigue, climate, and starvation. Olney felt "that a people coming from one country to fight another, have on the whole much the worst of it." [127] Occurrences, such as this often motivated the American cause and kept the soldiers in high spirits.

With the suffering of British troops acting as a motivational factor, soldiers such as Joseph Plumb Martin and George Robert Twelves Hewes felt the Americans suffered worse than the British with the lack of provisions the country could not afford to provide. Throughout their memoirs, there were often complaints of the suffering and hardships. As an officer, perhaps Stephen Olney fared better than his soldiers. Provisions needed to be adequately dispersed, even at the cost of the private soldiers.

During the war, several occurrences were depicted by Captain Olney that illuminated the motivations for not only his interests, but other soldiers as well. These motivations were both based on self-interests and a strong national identity emerging through desolation. Both the Americans and British were known to hold prisoners of war. However, the treatment of these soldiers was often scrutinized by both sides.

Captain Olney reiterated that his British prisoners were of "mature age, good sense, and very considerable information." [128] However, he was also astonished that "such persons should doubt the justice of the patriot cause, and still more astonishing that they avowed their belief that the States had not the means of supporting their independence." [129] Pride was a clear factor for Olney as he desperately wanted to prove Americans could be independent.

The American prisoners were known to have not fared as well, as mentioned by Colonel William Barton. Olney describes a situation when intelligence reached an American camp that American prisoners in New York were cruelly treated. It enraged the Americans when they heard their fellow comrades were "exposed to the inclemency of the weather, not allowed sufficient nourishment, even of the most sordid and repulsive kind, exposed to the insults of the soldiers, a shocking want of cleanliness." [130] Within a few weeks, around 1500 American troops perished from disease. The Royal officers attempted to convince the soldiers to join the British military, but they refused – showing their national identity. Those soldiers preferred death before joining the British military.

The imprisoned American officers fared no better as they "were escorted about street to be the sport of royal mob, and even beaten for daring to solicit some relief for their suffering soldiers, who were perishing for food and in the infected dungeons." [131] General Howe of the British military denied the allegations, but when Washington suggested sending an agent to provide for the men, Howe refused. The awful allegations caused Americans to go from sheer patriotism and love of country to utter hatred of the British. The American cause was bolstered by a motivation to save Americans from British prisons and to ensure others would not meet the same fate.

The revolutionary cause was also motivated by the reading of the Declaration of Independence around 1776 because it inspired men with the words "never to lay down her arms until these United States should be free, sovereign, and independent!" [132] However, there were times during the war that hope had faded. Olney recalled a meeting between two Captains who felt the country's probability of success was limited and decided it was impossible to win the war. Olney quickly offered his opinion to the contrary despite their experience. This was an instance in which Olney had to persuade fellow officers that independence was near, instead of providing inspiration to his troops. He often needed to provide motivation for the soldiers who were without adequate resources. On October 19, 1776, Olney had his first child and had a great desire to return home, but he would not be deterred from the war effort. [133]

When the campaign in New Jersey had ended, the troops were given the opportunity to rest at Morristown. Towards the end of 1777, Olney and other Rhode Island troops were granted leave and could return home to their families. The task of getting home was long and arduous - traveling on foot through part of Massachusetts and Connecticut.

Once he returned home, Olney recalled that he thought he "was clear of the army, but found I had been appointed a Captain in the second Rhode Island regiment, commanded by Colonel Israel Angell." [134] Olney described his pay as not nearly sufficient enough to pay his expenses. "I was in hopes," wrote Olney, "that a Captain's pay of 40 dollars per month, would yield me some remuneration, and as the American cause had become more desperate, it seemed like cowardice, and dishonorable to forsake my country now in distress, though many officers that had been brought up more delicately, had by the service already performed, become satisfied, and found their patriotism expended, and declined serving any longer." [135] Olney's statement marks an underlying theme that many officers sought economic incentive before displaying their patriotism. The author, Mrs. Williams, writes "an appeal to a man's pocket, excites more sensation than any thing else. Public spirit, patriotism, all fall before it." [136] For Olney, public spirit and patriotism were significant factors in defeating the British, but he was also expecting economic incentive for him to continue his service.

In June of 1778, Olney returned to camp at Peekskill, where he witnessed that thousands had been added to the army. This reinvigorated the troops and gave them a new sense of hope. The rumors of France reaching the country and fighting on behave of the Americans further reinvigorated the troops. The British strategy to burn houses and ravage the land did little to dissuade the American cause.

Captain Olney provides a small anecdote to the winter at Valley Forge, but according to the author, Mrs. Williams, he "says nothing of any suffering." [137] The winter at Valley Forge can be considered nothing short of a miracle that the Americans survived. Olney simply mentioned that "we drew a ration of salt pork and hard bread, and for the first time, I relished such food without the process of cooking, and even thought it delicious." He continued by stating that "for several days we had no rations at all, only parts of rations." [138] The horrors that many soldiers described at Valley Forge were not described in detail by Captain Olney.

Perhaps, Olney had bad memories and chose not to recount his experience or his situation was not as destitute as the private soldiers. It could also be the fact he left on furlough, about the first of January. He seemingly left for furlough because there were numerous mouths to feed, and there were a large proportion of officers to the men. That rationale suggests the officers were getting more rations than the private soldiers and he felt that he could be spared. From

1777-1778, Americans were not only facing dire circumstances, but they also had to battle both American merchants and farmers who placed a high economic value on their products.

During the war, Captain Olney was wounded twice, and after each time, he recovered and returned to the war. At the Battle of Springfield, he ordered his men to take possession of a small hill covered with wood and he was shot in the left arm with a rifle ball. After tying the wound off with a handkerchief, he thought it was best to retreat. He eventually made it to a hospital at Bearskin Ridge where he remained for eight to ten weeks for the wound to heal properly.

In 1779, Captain Olney, like many officers, had the luxury of returning home to visit his family. His second child, Joseph Olney, was born in 1779. The duty to his country prevailed over his familial duties and he soon left to rejoin his company in Yorktown, Virginia. He was fortunate enough to partake in the capitulation of Cornwallis in 1781.

Captain Olney stayed in the military for nearly the duration of the war, ending with the siege of Yorktown. He did not immediately end his commission after the siege of Yorktown as he waited until March 1782 to relinquish it. Once Cornwallis was captured, the fate of the British was conceded. After impeccable service to his country, Captain Olney left the army with distasteful feelings. An unhappy Olney stated "as I had suffered from the enemy's guns in front of battle, they (his brother officers) considered it as an imposition." [139] It was Olney's belief that "there are some who make it their business to pull down the character of others so much easier than to build up their own." [140] Olney felt many officers were careerists and manipulated the army for their own self-interests.

Olney appeared more than satisfied not being dependent on the British any longer. His performance in defending his country through the adversity and also to the satisfaction of his superiors was all he had expected from the war. He expected "no reward but the Independence and liberty of my country." [141] Being 27 years old, he sought to find another calling to support his growing family. Based on principle, he resigned his commission before the war had officially ended.

Benjamin Gilbert, another officer, received his commission in 1780. Shortly before, he had spent six months at home in Brookfield, Massachusetts. He began his military career as a private and sergeant for nearly four years before gaining his commission as an officer. Around 1780, it was his prerogative to be discharged and returned home in order "to indulge his sociable impulses." [142] While home, he enjoyed a time of leisure, instead of working. It appeared as though Gilbert was satisfied with not returning to the war. However, when he received orders to report back as a commissioned officer he took advantage of the opportunity.

Throughout the war, he was not particularly enthralled about being in the military. He often dealt with personal depression while in the military and seemed to have enjoyed a life of leisure. He had little motivation to participate in a war that appeared it had intruded on his life. The four years he served as a private and sergeant appeared to have demoralized his motivation to continue serving in the war.

Under the 1818 pension law, the first Federal welfare program, Gilbert had his pension approved. His pension application provided information on where he served and for whom he served. On April 19, 1775, he marched for Lexington and enlisted in Captain Peter Harwood's Company in Colonel Leonard's Regiment, serving in that regiment for two years. In January

1777, he enlisted in Captain Daniel Shays Company as a sergeant in the 5th Massachusetts Regiment commanded by Colonel Rufus Putnam, serving for two years. In the Campaign of 1779, he was then promoted to Ensign in Colonel Rufus Putnam's regiment. Finally, he was commissioned Lieutenant for the remainder of the war in 1782. [143] His pension application tracks his ranking throughout the military and enables him to earn the pay he deservedly earned.

During the last three years of the war, Benjamin Gilbert frequently corresponded with his family and friends. His service as an officer in the American army was highlighted in these letters. The year 1780 primarily consisted of letters that depicted his personal depression. This was at a time when the Americans were gaining control of the war.

On October 8, 1780, he wrote to his father and stepmother that despite their disagreeable situation with limited rations and supplies, the men were inspired by the treason of Benedict Arnold. For Gilbert, this gave reason to "the most convincing proof that the liberties of America is the object of divine protection." [144] Although some soldiers had deserted the American cause to receive a bounty from Benedict Arnold to join the British, it still did not deter the Americans. Gilbert wrote that he feared the consequences if they succeeded as "we should at once ben deprived of all communications with the New England State and must have perished or distressed the Inhabitants." [145] Essentially, Gilbert directly stated that the American cause was hindered by this situation with many fearing the consequences of their dissent. Ultimately, this situation would inspire many Americans as they believed in sovereignty from the British.

On January 2, 1781, he wrote to his brother in law Charles Bruce while at West Point describing the current situation within the American army. He made reference about the winter quarters as "still many Embarrassments occur which render our situation disagreeable." [146] He continued "our men are naked and not like to be clothed. Some have Received no money since December 1779, the others not since March 1780. Our wood is four miles to fetch by warter and then a bad hill which is equill to one mile more. Now I leave you Judg whether I am happy or not." [147] Congress could not financially afford to provide for their army and many soldiers became agitated with their situation.

Gilbert's hope for winning the war was wavering. As evidence, he wrote to his brother-in-law, "and in addition to my troubles, I have not received a letter from you since I left Brookfield," as he desired to hear what his "Domestick Buisiness" was like at home. [148] Gilbert was focused not on the war, but rather on life back home. On April 11, 1781, while stationed at Elkton, Maryland, Gilbert wrote to his father and stepmother that "our situation is pecularly unhappy as the troops that are with us have not drawn one half of their winter Cloths and received but one month pay for more than a year, and the People in this part of the Continent are not given to acts of Hospitallity. Therefore I think I shall be very unhappy in the Comand, and how I shall furnish myself with Cloths I know not." [149] Not only was Congress not helping with their situation, but the people in the country could ill-afford to help as well.

By September 19, 1781, while stationed near Williamsburg, Virginia, Gilbert wrote a letter to his father displaying his happiness. The French fleet had successfully surrounded and trapped Lord Cornwallis's army in Yorktown. Gilbert wrote "nothing but the warmest Expectations of capturing Cornwallis keeps my spirits hight, my Cloths being almost worne out, and no money to get new ones, having Received but 25 Dollars since March Eighty which passed six for one and no expectations of getting any sone." [150] Gilbert was motivated with the arrival of the French army. He had no hope for Congress to resupply the American army, but he expected an American victory with the newfound help of the French.

In a letter dated August 23, 1782, he wrote to his cousin Daniel Gould suggesting that peace negotiations appeared likely and that he would soon be discharged from the army. In this letter he also writes "I have received a Lieutenant's appointment in the 5th Massachusetts Regiment and am anexed to the Light Infantry Company." [151] Receiving a Lieutenant's commission seemed to have given Gilbert a higher spirit as the tone of his letters drastically changed from 1780. On August 24, 1782, he wrote to his father that "in consequence of the armies being kept without pay this summer a great number of Officers have resined which has made a Vacancy for Lieutenacy for me." [152] Gilbert believed that many officers felt they were underappreciated and deserved pay for their efforts. Gilbert, however, was happy to receive a commission as a Lieutenant.

The Siege of Yorktown in 1781 marked a turning point for Gilbert and the Americans. The revolution for Gilbert was one in which the war had intruded on his life and he appeared to have little desire to fight for his country. He appeared to be motivated by economic security when he received an officer's commission in 1780. Until 1780, it appeared unlikely that he would rejoin the army after serving as a private and sergeant for four years. Gilbert's experience for Gilbert regularly showed him as being demoralized by the lack of supplies and under-appreciation.

Like many of the private soldiers, these men joined the army to defend their country and display their patriotism, but also to enhance their economic and social standing. Each officer was motivated to join the war for his own reasons, but it appeared many were motivated for reasons other than national pride. These four men were able to secure social, economic, and political prominence in their respective post-revolution environments.

[102] Benjamin Tallmadge, *Memoir*, 9.

[103] Ibid., 9-10.

[104] Ibid., 15.

[105] Ibid., 16-17

[106] Ibid., 19.

[107] Ibid.

[108] Ibid., 33

[109] Williams, *Biography of Revolutionary Heroes*, 43.

[110] Ibid., 44.

[111] Ibid., 48.

[112] Ibid., 54-55.

[113] Ibid., 63.

[114] Ibid., 64.

[115] Ibid., 77.

[116] Ibid., 79.

[117] Ibid., 79-80.

[118] Ibid., 90.

[119] Ibid., 97.

[120] Ibid., 149-150.

[121] Ibid., 150.

[122] Ibid.

[123] Ibid., 153.

[124] Ibid., 158.

[125] Ibid., 159.

[126] Ibid.

[127] Ibid., 161.

[128] Ibid., 163.

[129] Ibid.

[130] Ibid., 186-187.

[131] Ibid., 187.

[132] Ibid., 164.

[133] Ibid., 185.

[134] Ibid., 202.

[135] Ibid., 202-203.

[136] Ibid., 236.

[137] Ibid., 233.

[138] Ibid.

[139] Ibid., 284.

[140] Ibid., 285.

[141] Ibid., 286.

[142] Shy, *Winding Down: the Revolutionary War letters of Lieutenant Benjamin Gilbert of Massachusetts*, 19.

[143] Ibid. 110.

[144] Ibid., 22.

[145] Ibid., 23.

[146] Ibid., 32.

[147] Ibid.

[148] Ibid.

[149] Ibid., 40-41.

[150] Ibid., 49.

[151] Ibid., 62.

[152] Ibid., 63.

Chapter Four

Post-Revolution: Soldiers and Their Transition to Peacetime

The peace settlement with the British in 1783, created a struggle with the transition to peacetime for both, the lowest and highest ranks of the military. These high expectations were soon met with dissent and deception. Despite making ill-advised promises to entice all able-bodied men to join the war effort, the newly formed American government was not equipped to provide for the economic needs of the soldiers.

After sacrificing their lives, the private soldiers soon realized the government had exploited them to achieve victory. Many soldiers would come to resent and disapprove of the government as they came to the realization that their leaders were deceiving them. Regardless, various attitudes and expectations were displayed by the soldiers after the war. This chapter will aim to shed light on how the eight men discussed above served their country transitioned to peacetime.

The private soldiers had a difficult time adjusting to life after the war. On April 19, 1783, Martin and his fellow soldiers received word that the British had capitulated and the Americans had gained independence. Martin recollected that the soldiers "were more closely fixed upon their situation as it respected the figure they were to exhibit upon their leaving the army and becoming citizens." [153] The men were as Martin observed "starved, ragged, and meagre" when the war closed. [154] They expressed deep apprehension at the thought of becoming citizens with no financial standing. Martin slowly realized that it was time for their brotherhood to come to an end, and they would need to utilize the same virtue of necessity that enabled them to withstand the sufferings of war. The soldiers were discharged and to the chagrin of Martin, the government had let them go in their "pitiful forlorn condition." [155]

Some of the men were able to get final settlement certificates, which they sold out of necessity to get clothing and money. Others just went back home with nothing. Martin was offered sixteen dollars in specie by another soldier who desperately wanted out of the regiment and he agreed. He would spend a short time more in the army to get an honorable discharge, and his final settlement certificates. After that Martin hastily stated, "I now bid a farewell to the service." [156] Martin seemed reluctant to leave the army and his comrades. After all, outside of working on his grandfather's farm as a young boy, the army was his life for eight years.

When traveling back to his home, he came across an army friend. Martin stopped and worked in the farming business for what was supposed to be a few days. However, with winter approaching, he agreed to stay to be a teacher. He taught a class of around twenty to thirty students and mentioned "I knew but little and they less, if possible." [157] Much like being in the army, Martin adapted to his surroundings and did the unimaginable. After the winter, he decided it was time to move on. By 1784, Martin would make his to Maine where he would spend the rest of his life until his death in 1850.

Martin believed the government was too powerful and caused even more of a socioeconomic imbalance for the enlisted soldiers. The government promised the enlisted soldiers one hundred acres of land each, in their own state, but they were quickly shunned at the prospect of this. The government also promised them ample supplies - clothing, food, and pay for joining the service - but they received little to none of those items. Martin noted that "the truth was, none cared for them; the country was served, and faithfully served, and that was all that was deemed necessary." [158] Martin suggested the least the government could have done was provide food for the demoralized soldiers.

Martin was considered an anti-Federalist because the government, as he saw it, did not support the people. Martin was enraged by the little remuneration he received during the course of the war. He stated "had I been paid as I was promised to be at my engaging in the service, I needed not to have suffered as I did, nor would I have done it." [159] Economic incentive was a motivational factor for Martin remaining in the army, but he also felt he was promised a better future and that was not fulfilled. He had a limited education and the war had consumed his youthful days. His hatred for the government became evident throughout his memoir. Martin concluded the government "had all the power in her hands, and I had none. Such things ought not to be." [160] Martin would go on to become a respected farmer on Maine's frontier. He also served as selectman, justice of the peace, and town clerk. Martin appeared to be a man of the people and sought to protect their interests.

The transition to peacetime was a difficult experience for Hewes and his family. He had entered the war poor and left poor. His hopes of striking it rich through the war were shattered. In the fall of 1832, his pension was approved, but at that point in his life did little. Hewes deemed the pension process as "long and expensive." [161] It does not appear he shared the same hatred for the government as Martin, but he was hoping for more of an economic recognition.

Hewes, like many others in New England, moved west in search of opportunity. Many believed the revolution would offer an opportunity to acquire higher social standing and respect. However, for men, such as Hewes, moving west was the only hope they had left.

On November 5, 1840, George Robert Twelves Hewes died. [162] He was considered a hero to many around the New England area. Hewes's memory lived on through various histories of the nation, the Revolution, and descendents naming their children and grandchildren after him. His patriotism was displayed by his personal experiences as he dispelled the notion of deference within society. For Hewes, the Revolution was an opportunity to show that lower class individuals could have the same effect in determining the outcome of the war as the upper class.

The transition to peacetime for John Greenwood was not difficult as he relocated to New York City. He realized that after the war he would have to acquire a trade or career. Although Greenwood never went beyond an elementary education, he did have "a zest for doing things that he enjoyed." [163] He would go on to repair watches, compasses, barometers, and complicated types of mathematical instruments. He also became a merchant and tried his skill as a wood turner, where he produced hickory walking canes. As early as 1784, Greenwood had acquired "a rudimentary knowledge of dentistry" from his father, John Greenwood, who began a practice in New York. [164] Before the war, he was apprehensive about joining the military, but the war became a life altering experience for him.

Greenwood was the rare example of not being compelled to ask the government for economic relief because of his struggles during the war. Once the war was over, he became determined to live his life to the fullest. Pride was a major factor for Greenwood because he could not ask his newly formed country to support.

As one of the most respected dentists among his contemporaries, Greenwood served George Washington's dental needs. His mechanical skills allowed him to build dentures for Washington. In 1806, he sailed to Paris, where he acquired knowledge on recent dental innovations that were unheard of in America. He was able to pioneer "the use of foot-power drills" and "adaptable springs for dentures." [165] He also began using hippopotamus ivory to formulate porcelain teeth.

Among other endeavors, he was a proponent of transplants from one human to another. He used this theory to replace decaying teeth with replacement teeth that he would purchase from other people. As a leading dentist, his practice flourished after he advertised in the New York Gazette that he was the "Dentist to His Excellency George Washington." [166] After the war, it was obvious that Greenwood was not prepared to sit idly and recollect the harsh memories he experienced from the war. He was the epitome of a soldier transitioning to peacetime with great success.

When he reached the age of sixty, his health began to fail as he suffered from a stroke of apoplexy. On November 16, 1819, Dr. John Greenwood would die at his residence. His two sons, Isaac John and Clark, would continue to operate the successful business that he commenced. The Dean of the Baltimore College of Dental Surgery, W.R. Handy described John Greenwood as being "the Father of American Dentistry as well as the Dentist of the Illustrious Father of our glorious Republic." [167] John Greenwood did not expect the war to propel him socially in post-war America. Transitioning to peacetime was difficult, but Greenwood was successful under harrowing circumstances.

The transition to peacetime for the twenty five year old Jeremiah Greenman was filled with high expectations as an established officer. He believed with his high ranking in the military that he deserved a distinguishable position. Much to his chagrin, the army was in the process of downsizing. Having his expectations deflated, Greenman saw his hard-work in the army as a waste. After the war, Greenman claimed that "having Devoted my youthful days to the service of my country I was deprived of the opportunity which young men generally possess of acquiring any mechanical art of perfecting my self in any profession." [168] He believed, like many other officers after the war, that he earned the republican virtue of having land awaiting him. As many soldiers were still young, they fully expected to finish "growing up with the country." [169] The country was young itself, which only complicated matters.

Greenman began his military career as a private, but worked his way through the military ranks. In the military, he learned how to keep accurate rolls and accounts, as well as analyzing and leading men. He quickly realized those skills would enable him to attempt transitioning from the military without governmental assistance. Many Revolutionary veterans took advantage of the congressional promises of bounty lands in the West.

Greenman, however, decided to challenge himself to make a living in Providence, Rhode Island. Providence was rapidly growing and full of promise in the 1780s. Newport, was once the metropolitan center of trade, saw half the population leave after British occupation in 1776. Providence's thriving commerce attracted Greenman and Joseph Masury, who were friends that had risen through the military ranks together in Olney's Rhode Island Battalion. In April of 1784, Greenman "entered into a contract with Mr. Masury to put our small Interest togeth[er], (which we had been fighting, bleeding, and all most dying for, - for the Space of 8 long years in the Army of the United States,) in order for to trade and try for a livelyhood." [170] The "small interest" that Greenman refers to "consisted of the five years' full pay that Congress had authorized for officers in lieu of half pay for life." [171] Greenman was fortunate enough to receive pay during the war for his services. Many soldiers received limited or no pay at all.

He ended the war as a first lieutenant serving as regimental adjutant, and receiving thirty-nine dollars a month. The sum of money that Greenman was receiving was significant enough to have his expectations raised by the end of the war. The military was all he knew and he had made the most of that opportunity.

By opening a retail shop, Greenman and Masury attempted to create a livelihood for themselves. Once they reached an agreement on the shop, Greenman went back to Swansea, Massachusetts as he was "fixing for to move my mother and Go[o]ds to Providenc." He believed his decision to move to Providence offered the most opportunity for the future. By the sixth day of April, the two men had begun their shop and "whent into traid." After a short time, their retail shop did not prosper as they envisioned. By September, Greenman realized that retail was not for him, especially when "business grow'd very dull." He tried unsuccessfully to make a livelihood with his friend. Greenman stated, "parted and trid a Shop and took my part of the stock and continued in the Mercantile line till Septr. 1785." [172] He continued to make a living in the mercantile business for another year.

Jeremiah married Mary Eddy on October 23, 1784. The Eddy family came to Providence during the postwar years and dominated the shipwright's craft. [173] Now that Greenman was married, the pressure of making a livelihood became more transparent. In late 1785, Greenman undertook a life at sea. He had studied navigation during the war, but the connection with the Eddy family only helped him. At 26 years old, Greenman planned on earning a captain's or master's position in the merchant business. To achieve that he would need to sail and learn from the bottom up. His first voyage came as a seaman aboard the *Active* for Boston, which was bound for the West Indies. [174] After traveling "to the Caneries & Cape Verd[e] Islands" and then dropping their cargo off in NewYork, he went back to Boston where he returned home to

Providence for a month. [175] The year at sea afforded little time for him to spend with his family. His first daughter, Mary Eddy Greenman, was born on November 26, 1785. [176]

The next voyage for Greenman would come aboard the *America*, which was bound "for the coast of Guin[e]a." [177] He earned a master's certificate during his two year voyage that allowed him to begin captaining the vessels. When he arrived back at Providence in May of 1788, his career was beginning to succeed. Socially, this was a job that Greenman enjoyed because "American shipmasters [were] received into the upper bourgeois society of the seaports where they traded." [178] Greenman would begin what became a fifteen year career as a sea captain in the merchant marine business.

One of Greenman's goals was to obtain a position in the United States Army with new companies being formed in each state. He would use his connection, Jeremiah Olney, who was his regimental commander to help achieve a position. Greenman wanted to become a captain in the army and leave the seas behind. He was denied the position with hundreds of other hopeful veterans competing for a government appointment. Greenman, then desired to become a first mate "on a revenue cutter" that would be bound for duty in Long Island Sound. [179]

Greenman was denied "first mate," but Olney's influence secured him "the Station of Second Mate" position. Greenman reluctantly accepted the position out of economic necessity. Greenman did not falter, despite being denied several times for governmental positions. The seafaring merchant business enabled Greenman and his family of five, and expecting a sixth, to become proprietors. They bought a lot and house for the "sum of one hundred and thirty five pounds Silver Lawful Money." [180] The Greenman family would remain at the estate for thirteen years. In 1799, Greenman became half-owner of the schooner *Jerushia*. After being shipmaster

for nearly all of 1800, he decided to sell his portion of the ship.

By 1806, a new opportunity emerged in the life of Jeremiah Greenman. With his health

deteriorating, from a wound associated with the war, Greenman decided to move west. He

decided to make use of his Revolutionary War land bounty, even though his family had a limited

knowledge of farming. His sons had urged him to use the claim as they wanted to attempt

farming. The Greenmans would sell their home in Providence for a profitable "1,000 Spanish

milled dollars," to take westward. [181]

The Greenman family moved to Marietta, Ohio. By 1806, Ohio had reached the sixty

thousand inhabitants that were required under the Northwest Ordinance of 1787 to allow

statehood. Greenman's rank of lieutenant entitled him to two hundred acres of land. Soon after,

he bought a small farm about fifteen miles north of Marietta, in a village called Waterford. He

called his property an "upland hilly farm," but was not considered desirable farm land. [182]

Greenman left the farm duties to his son Jeremiah. He would pass time by reading and taking

walks, and occasionally riding by horse to Waterford to interact with the townspeople.

Greenman was also elected the justice of the peace a few times and he held an official public

position between 1812 and 1816. With that position, he was able to marry couples, witness

lesser legal documents, and keep an "estray book" of lost and wandering horses. [183] Through

these various activities, the Greenman family increasingly dealt with poverty. He was well-

respected in the community and helped found the Freemasons in Waterford.

The year of 1818 was a breakthrough for many Revolutionary veterans as the Pension

Act was approved by Congress. It was a life pension that granted officers twenty dollars monthly (eight dollars for private soldiers) "who served in the War of the Revolution until the end thereof, of for the term of nine months…on the continental establishment." [184] On April 16, 1818, Greenman went to court and was granted a pension. However, by 1820, Congress believed some were taking advantage of the system. The amendatory act of May 1820 forced those pensioners to prove their reduced circumstances by providing a list of personal property and income.

It became clear that Greenman and his wife were living in reduced circumstances, as he recalls only having sixty dollars to their names. That money was gained from the two years of being on the pension roll. In a letter written to the Secretary of War, Greenman stated "in my old age and inabilities to persue my occupation as a farmer, will afford me some degree of suppor, without th[r]owing myself on the charrity of my Children, which has been the case for five years before I received the bounty of my country." He believed that after "Eight years & Siven Months service together with three wounds received whist in that service" he deserved compensation from the government. [185]

In his last appeal to Congress on September 20, 1821, Greenman finally persuaded the War Department to re-establish his pension. Being sixty three years old, his health was declining and he was unable to work hard labor on the farm. He made sure to make these points throughout a well-drawn letter to the War Department. He also reiterated the fact that some veterans received a pension after only participating in the war for a limited time. He mentioned how his neighbor only served for a "short duration, but long enough to come under the period of time allowed of by Law to intitle him to a pension, but he hath frequently told Me that, he was tired of the Service & that he had hired a substitute, & for all I know both receive the bounty of their country." [186] He was forced to defend his honor and righteousness after defending his country for the duration of the war.

After winning the long battle with Washington over his pension, he was now content to live the remainder of his life without regret. Politically in 1828, he voted for John Quincy Adams which brought back his New England roots. His roots were predicated upon the virtue of self-reliance. One month after he voted for Adams, he passed away at his home on November 15, 1828. The citizenry of Waterford came to his funeral in large numbers and he was buried on his "upland hilly farm" where his grave still rests.

Soon after his death, the Greenman family decided to sell the property and move westward to Illinois to farm better land. The widow Greenman continued to receive Jeremiah's pension until her passing in 1839. The obituary of Jeremiah Greenman suggested he was "an orphan boy, and had no influential connexions." [187] Being an orphan boy with no influential connections, he proved that it was possible to move up the social ladder in society.

Transitioning to peacetime was not as difficult for many officers. Officers were able to adjust – socially, politically, and economically – by using their military standing. Although some officers, such as Lt. Benjamin Gilbert were unsure of the available opportunities it would prove easier for them than the private soldiers.

In a letter to his cousin Daniel Gould on November 16, 1782, Gilbert concluded "as a Millitary calling is my present support, I think it more Eligible to persue it than to submit to a Political Death." [188] Gilbert envisioned his future would rest in a military capacity since it offered social and economic standing. In June of 1783, he wrote to his father "as I am about to retire from the Military Theatre to walks of private life, without any cash, or the means of obtaining any, I find it necessary to make some arrangements for my future support." [189] A sense

of despair set in as the military could no longer provide for him. He was fortunate to have a

father whom he could rely on for financial stability unlike many other soldiers.

In 1786, shortly after the war, Gilbert would marry Molly Cornwall. She was the

daughter of Captain John Cornwall of Danbury, Connecticut. Gilbert and Molly would

eventually have eleven children together.

The war had taken away any opportunity for many soldiers to receive an education. The

town of Brookfield offered limited opportunities, which caused Gilbert to relocate to a more

vibrant town. Brookfield was described as "rural beyond almost any other town in the region."

[190] Gilbert relocated to Albany, New York and then to Middlefield, a town just east of Ostego

Lake. He began his new life as a teacher and would purchase a farm near Cherry Valley.

In October 1786, Gilbert was commissioned Adjutant by Colonel Cannon in a New York

militia regiment. Six years later, he was elected as Sheriff of Ostego County, New York. He also

served three terms as assemblyman in the New York State legislature, and held numerous local

and county offices. Gilbert was a staunch supporter of Federalist principles and supported a

strong government. Despite not wanting to submit to a "political death," Gilbert was interested

in politics. [191] He was also a member of a Masonic Lodge. At 72 years old, Benjamin Gilbert

passed away on January 18, 1828. The life of Benjamin Gilbert was illuminated by the candid

letters to his family and friends about his Revolutionary War experiences and personal life.

The transition to peacetime proved less difficult for Benjamin Tallmadge. After the war,

Benjamin married Mary Floyd, the daughter of William Floyd who was a signer of the

Declaration of Independence and a member of the Continental Congress for nine years.

Benjamin and Mary were joined in matrimony on March 16, 1784 at her home in Mastic, Long Island, New York. She was just twenty years old, while Benjamin was thirty. Soon after, the couple moved to Litchfield, Connecticut.

Benjamin and Mary needed assistance with their new home in Litchfield and "purchased two Negro boys in 1784 and 1785." With the extra help, Mary was able to settle in comfortably and created a home worthy of not only her ambitions, but also her husband's. Benjamin and Mary's first child, William Smith Tallmadge, was born on October 20, 1785. Benjamin convinced his friend in Long Island, Ezra L'Hommedieu to sell a Negro slave girl named Jane to him for 36 pounds lawful money to provide more assistance to his growing family. The thirteen year old slave girl was acquired on "March 10, 1787, shortly before the birth of Henry Floyd Tallmadge." [192] As the Tallmadge family grew, so did their social standing in Litchfield.

Benjamin had forged a strong reputation in Litchfield. However, he sought to become more politically involved, not just in Litchfield, but nationally. After the war had ended, he began a prosperous mercantile business called "B. Tallmadge & Company." [193] In April of 1797, Benjamin and Mary welcomed their sixth child into the family. With the increased pressure of Mary to take care of six children, Benjamin brokered an agreement with a couple from Holland. Benjamin had paid $157 for their passage and they would work for three years during their indenture and for each additional child born during their term an additional six months more. On September 13, 1800 (at the end of their three year term), Benjamin and Mary welcomed their seventh child, George Washington Tallmadge causing the indenture to remain for an additional six months.

Benjamin was involved in numerous activities and investments after the war. He was an ambitious man who sought political and economic advancement. He joined the Connecticut Society of the Cincinnati in 1783 and was one of the original members. The society enabled him to gain political strength as it played a significant role within state politics.

In 1785, he was elected assistant treasurer and four years later he was made treasurer. While he served as treasurer, his friend and prominent figure, Jeremiah Wadsworth, was president. Wadsworth was a prominent member of the House of Representatives and supported a strong federal government. Benjamin was able to further develop his career by having Wadsworth as a connection. Benjamin was also treasurer for the Ohio Company of Associates, which enhanced his financial abilities. In 1790, while in Litchfield, Connecticut he became a "lister or assessor" for the town. [194] By 1791, he was "made claim commissioner for Litchfield County." [195] Then, once Congress voted to extend mail service into western Connecticut in 1792, Benjamin was named postmaster of Litchfield. He was also named a county commissioner and in 1794 he was elected as town treasurer, based on his financial expertise. He was eventually named president of the Connecticut Society of the Cincinnati. By 1801, Benjamin was known nationally through his various positions.

He was a supporter of John Adams, not Thomas Jefferson, because he was unsure of Virginia's intentions. He also supported the Alien and Sedition Acts and opposed the Democrats. After years of building his reputation, he finally secured a position in the House of Representatives (defeating his opponent by over three thousand votes) in the fall of 1801. He relinquished his town duties and went to the national capital. In 1805, his wife had passed away, at age 41, and his relationship with his children became stronger. He often wrote his favorite daughter, Maria, and continuously encouraged all of his children to correspond with him. In

1807, he became a member of the Ways and Means Committee, after being defeated for House Speaker. After numerous years on the Ways and Means Committee, he soon decided to become a member of the Committee of Commerce and Manufacturers.

Despite Benjamin's active political career, he married for a second time to Maria Hallett, who was the daughter of a prominent merchant. She was twenty two years younger than Benjamin, but she blended well into the Litchfield home and secured the respect of his children. Congress needed to raise money by taxation because of the War of 1812 and Benjamin with his financial experience was appointed to the Committee on the Military Establishment. The committee "tried to bring some order out of the chaotic condition of the war effort." [196] By 1816, Tallmadge decided to leave his name off the Federalist ticket because of his age (62 years old) and his health was declining. Benjamin used his military standing to his advantage by becoming an influential businessman and political figure.

The post-war life for Colonel William Barton was one of social prominence. Once the war had ended, he had fathered seven sons and two daughters who were all educated "in good moral principles and industrious habits." [197] Barton sought to keep his children sober, industrious, and useful citizens. After fighting for independence, Barton often referred to aristocrats as "trash". [198] He shunned those of the gentry who were seeking to rule the newly formed American society.

Despite earning social prominence, Barton, unlike many officers, was not considered wealthy at any time. About fifteen years before his death he was involved in a lawsuit in Vermont. It was in consequence of his purchase of the township within the state called "Barton," in the county of Orleans. This town was then purchased by the state of Vermont, instead of being a gift of the United States to Barton. His title to the piece of land was disputed in the court

of law and he was ordered to pay, but he found the demand to be unconstitutional and refused to

pay it. "With him," according to the author, "his word was final." [199] For his actions, he was

sued, and detained in the town of Danville, in Caledonia County, for fourteen years. He had

resigned himself to the town and seemingly enjoyed life at a hotel where he was boarded.

When he was detained, he never imagined seeing home again. That all changed in 1824,

when Lafayette, a friend from the revolution heard of his predicament and desired to help.

Lafayette believed that Barton served his country faithfully and shouldn't be forced to suffer with

indignation. Lafayette sent a messenger to pay the debt and Barton was free. When Barton

arrived back home, Lafayette and other veterans, were there to congratulate him.

After Lafayette secured Barton's freedom, Barton quickly realized that his self-devotion

and patriotism had not been forgotten. On October 22, 1831, a few years after returning home,

Colonel William Barton died at the age of 85. "The immediate cause of death," wrote Mrs.

Williams, "was a fit of apoplexy, which he survived only a few days, and from which his mind

never recovered, as he was perfectly insensible to all around him, from the moment of attack, to

that of his death." [200] Mrs. Williams wrote, "he was a person of old fashioned notions, and old

fashioned politeness." [201] Despite a lack of education, Barton achieved success with sheer

determination.

Barton promoted a harmonious society and repudiated the aristocracy because it opposed

the revolutionary ideal of republicanism. Mrs. Williams noted Barton would have said, "to get

rid of these paltry things (aristocratic notions), we took up arms, and shall we after shedding our

blood to be free, bow down our necks again to the yoke of bondage." [202] For his devotion, the

Secretary of War, Hon. Mr. J. Knox, sent a letter to Barton on August 1, 1786 stating that he would receive a sword - "very fine workmanship; the blade of tempered steel, silver hilted, chased with gold, in emblematical devices, and the words, "Gift of Congress to Colonel Barton 25th July, 1777" - for making prisoners of Prescott and Major Barrington, his aide de camp. [203] The sword, worth $100 at the time, was still being preserved in the Barton family when this book was written. On August 10, 1786 deflected any accomplishment, and instead praised the bravery and "unshaken firmness" of his soldiers. [204] Many viewed Barton as benevolent, modest, and determined. The Barton family was considered highly respectable with their residence being two miles from the village of Warren, at a place called Barton's Point.

Captain Stephen Olney had a similar transition to peacetime as Barton as they were both modest and benevolent. Olney chose to settle into relative obscurity on his farm in Rhode Island. The townsmen, however, had other plans for their war hero. They elected him their Representative for numerous years in the State Legislature, and President of the Town-Council. Olney was able to use his military standing to achieve political success. It was Olney's honor, however, to serve in both offices and he did so with the acceptance of the townspeople. Olney and his wife would have a total of eight children, one of which he affectionately named him "George Washington." [205] Olney's wife died on December 13, 1813.

Thirteen years after his wife's death, he married a widow in Johnston, Rhode Island. His second wife insisted for him to stay with her on her farm in Johnston for the remaining years of his life. Throughout this time period, Captain Olney was persistent in his attempt to acquire a pension. He wrote in a letter "I was about 6 years and ten month in the army." He deserved compensation as a soldier and officer. After the war, he modestly spoke in terms of not receiving any compensation, as independence and liberty were enough for him. However, in

May of 1828 when the pension act passed, intended "for the relief of those who served until the end of the war, not extending to his case," he sought to petition for a pension. [206] Olney wrote "my petition enumerates the principal causes that induced me to leave the army." [207] He left the army because of anger toward "a set of miscreants who if they cannot build up themselves, will be seeking to pull down all above them." [208] Olney felt other officers were taking advantage of the military in order to boost their own self-interests. With that, in 1782, he resigned his commission.

In another letter, Olney wrote "my case being singular, and my services so near similar to those officers who served till peace, that I could not help entertaining the pleasing hopes that Congress, in their liberality, would grant me the like remuneration, the pay to commence when theirs did." [209] On May 28, 1830 (two years after the pension act passed), Olney secured a pension. His situation "complied with all the requisitions of the fourth section." [210] Olney fought desperately for a pension because he had eight children and twenty six grandchildren to help provide for. When he reached 75 years old, Olney suffered with a cancerous tumor and felt he owed his family to reap the benefits from serving his country.

On November 23, 1832, aged 77, Captain Stephen Olney departed this life. A short time before his death, Olney traveled back to his farm, by his own request, where he remained until his death. He was buried on his farm in North-Providence where a slate stone records his name and a brief history of his services during the revolution. After being twice wounded in the revolution, Olney was extremely proud to fight for his country and expected nothing from the country in return. It was not until his later life that he sought to be remunerated for his services, but he did so with his family in mind.

Part of Olney's obituary read "Another Hero and Patriot of the Revolution departed! He was in the best and highest sense of the words, a Patriot and a Republican, devotedly attached to our national institutions and interests, for which in his younger days, he had so often been ready to make the sacrifice of his life. He constantly toiled with his own hands, and the testimony of his untiring industry and perseverance, and sterling integrity, is fresh in the remembrance of all who knew him." [211] Like his Rhode-Island comrade, Colonel William Barton, both had won the respect of their peers.

[153] Martin, *A Narrative of a Revolutionary Soldier*, 239-240.

[154] Ibid., 240.

[155] Ibid.

[156] Ibid., 242.

[157] Ibid., 243.

[158] Ibid., 244.

[159] Ibid., 247.

[160] Ibid.

[161] Young. *The Shoemaker and the Tea Party*, 67-68.

[162] Ibid., 76.

[163] Greenwood, *The Wartime Services of John Greenwood*, 149.

[164] Ibid., 149.

[165] Ibid., 150.

[166] Ibid.

[167] Ibid., 151.

[168] Greenman, *Diary of a Common Soldier*, xiv.

[169] Ibid., xv-xvi.

[170] Ibid., 273.

[171] Ibid., xvii.

[172] Ibid., 273.

[173] Ibid., xviii.

[174] Ibid., 273.

[175] Ibid.

[176] Ibid., xix.

[177] Ibid., 273.

[178] Ibid., xx.

[179] Ibid., xxi.

[180] Ibid., xxii.

[181] Ibid., xxiv.

[182] Ibid., 293.

[183] Ibid., xxvii.

[184] Ibid., xxix.

[185] Ibid., 296.

[186] Ibid., 298.

[187] Ibid., 306.

[188] Shy, ed., *Winding Down: the Revolutionary War letters of Lieutenant Benjamin Gilbert*, 72.

[189] Ibid., 106.

[190] Ibid., 100.

[191] Ibid., 72.

[192] Hall, *Benjamin Tallmadge: Revolutionary Soldier and American Businessman*, 95.

[193] Ibid., 96.

[194] Ibid., 162.

[195] Ibid., 165.

[196] Ibid., 224.

[197] Williams, Biography of Revolutionary Heroes, 97.

[198] Ibid., 98.

[199] Ibid.

[200] Ibid., 102.

[201] Ibid., 105.

[202] Ibid., 107-108.

[203] Ibid., 111.

[204] Ibid., 112.

[205] Ibid., 287.

[206] Ibid., 290.

[207] Ibid., 291.

[208] Ibid.
[209] Ibid., 293.
[210] Ibid., 295.
[211] Ibid., 297.

Conclusion

The idea of meeting another set of challenges as the American Revolution soldiers transitioned to peacetime was met with much discontent and fear. After all, according to many, they had suffered enough during the war without receiving much compensation. For many, the transitions were difficult, but most were able to find some semblance within their lives. Some became prosperous, others ended the war the same way they started: in poverty. The war for many meant an opportunity to prove their capabilities as they sought to impress their superiors. Opportunity became a lasting motivational factor for many soldiers because they viewed the American Revolution as a way to improve their position in society.

Throughout this comparative study, it became evident that each of these men were motivated to join and stay in the war for their own reasons. New England was faced with a unique situation as many soldiers were essentially forced into the military because of dwindling opportunities and poverty. John Shy argued "the ranks were being filled with lower class individuals who were joining the war for the wrong reasons; money, escape, and assurance of easy discipline and this caused the more respectable men to shy away from joining as they felt not so impelled by a sense of duty." [212] These men were also attracted to the Continental Army by the affluence, comfort, security, and prestige that came with being in the military.

Congress promised bounties to each soldier for enlisting in the war, which was advantageous for many, especially lower class individuals. Another factor was lower class individuals envisioned the military as an opportunity to influence politics, but not dominate them. This would ultimately lead to a democracy in America being created. While the lower class individuals were attempting to influence politics, upper class men began to develop a political consciousness, which became prevalent during and after the revolution.

Many officers of the revolution went on to further their political consciousness by competing for positions locally and nationally as they transitioned to peacetime. For many officers, winning the war meant securing positions that were based on their own self-interests. On the other hand, the private soldiers were fighting to destroy inequality within their society. Once they joined the war, it gave them a new sense of citizenship and personal worth that enabled them to denounce deference.

The main goal of the Revolution for both private soldiers and officers was to win the war. If winning the war was to become attainable, then both groups could reap the benefits. Through this research, it appeared that each side had reason to be motivated to win the war. Each side was motivated to secure their own self-interests.

During the war, the soldiers experienced numerous hardships and deprivation as they not only had to worry about enemy, but also their own government. In a war that must have seemed would never end, the only way to win, according to Edward Countryman, "required the willingness of thousands of very ordinary men in the ranks to put up with disease, danger, physical conditions that often were horrifying." [213] Shy argued that Americans won the war due to the gradual decline of American support after 1775 because they kept the people engaged long enough to discourage the British. Shy maintained "that support declined over the next six years and people seemed to be getting tired of the long war, which inadvertently and ironically benefited them in obtaining independence because they were able to hang on long enough to discourage the British Government and people." [214] Both arguments by Countryman and Shy coincide with the eight men in this study and their motivations for joining, as well as staying in the war.

After winning the war, both sides appeared to express disappointment in the government. Their expectations were not immediately met by Congress because of an American economy that was experiencing rapid inflation. Many were seeking economic value for their services, particularly the private soldiers, since they had a limited means to support themselves. Allan Bowman argued that despite their differing motivations "American morale was high in one aspect, which was their devotion to the cause as they were able to maintain fortitude through long periods of hardships." [215] It is undeniable the American Revolution was considered "a time that tried men's souls," but both the private soldiers and officers were able to coexist to win the war.

The motivations and experiences of both the private soldiers and officers in New England helped to upset the equilibrium in revolutionary society. It went from working harmoniously together to a competing society based on one's own self-interests. This became evident in the stories of these eight men. Their motivations and experiences would ultimately help create the society as America knows today.

---

[212] John Shy, *A People Numerous and Armed: Reflections on the Military Struggle for American Independence* (New York: Oxford University Press, 1976), 30-31.

[213] Edward Countryman, *The American Revolution* (New York: Hill and Wang, 2003), 136.

[214] John Shy, *A People Numerous and Armed*, 13-14.

[215] Allan Bowman, *The Morale of the American Revolutionary Army* (New York: Kennikat Press, 1964), 57.

www.ingramcontent.com/pod-product-compliance
Lightning Source LLC
LaVergne TN
LVHW041340200726
843509LV00009B/800